happy trails

The Story of
ROY ROGERS
and
DALE EVANS

happy
trails

with
Carlton Stowers

WORD BOOKS
PUBLISHER
WACO, TEXAS

HAPPY TRAILS

Library of Congress Catalog Card Number:
ISBN 0–8499–0086–7
Printed in the United States of America.

First Printing: October 1979
Second Printing: November 1979

Dedication

To Art, without whom this book could not have been written.

William Arthur Rush, our manager, agent and friend for lo, these thirty-one years of "Happy Trails," and even before . . . The Bible says: "There is a friend that sticketh closer than a brother"—you are that friend to us, Art.

The three of us have experienced "a whole pitcher" of public life together. We have weathered some incredibly rough storms in our personal lives and careers. We have flown on the wings of success, and sometimes landed in defeat. Despite the degree of turbulence, we chose to "hang in there together," with faith in God and each other.

You enrolled for a pre-med course at Bethany College, but switched emphasis midstream, toward an AB degree, probably prompted by the long inner desire to be in the entertainment industry. You came to Hollywood in 1932 and hit your stride quickly as top executive in recording and artist management.

You were the first Hollywood person to speak to me, Dale, of God. "How strange," I thought at the time,"for a Hollywood agent to speak of God and prayer!" But it registered.

Though you are not a preacher, your exemplary life has preached to all of us who know you.

Thank you, Art and your lovely Mary Jo, for the guidance, understanding, support and friendship.
We love you.

Dale and Roy

*Roy, if you had to thank God for
one thing, what would that be?*

"The mountains and the valleys.
If there were no valley of sadness
and death, we could never
really appreciate the sunshine
of happiness on the mountaintop."

—from a 1975 interview with
   Roy Rogers by Joe Curreri

Contents

Foreword

To THOSE OF US eleven-going-on-twelve, it was a simpler time. Life's great challenges revolved around how to pass to the sixth grade, avoid girls, and scrape up the necessary nine cents cash each week for the Saturday afternoon matinee down at the Bijou. There in the cool, popcorn-scented darkness of our rural West Texas theater, we could escape for a few hours from the yoke of clinging little sisters and bullying big brothers and joyfully ride alongside Roy Rogers as he went about his weekly business of stomping the living what-for out of evil, righting wrongs, and singing his way into the heart of his lady-friend Dale Evans who, for a girl, wasn't too bad inasmuch as she seemed to think as highly of Roy as we did.

Indeed, if my childhood ever acquainted me with a true-life Ward of Heaven, Roy Rogers, King of the Cowboys, was that person.

Needless to say, I was hardly alone in my unabashed hero worship. In the years between 1943 and 1954 Roy Rogers was annually voted Hollywood's number one money-making Western star. Over four hundred merchandising products bearing his endorsement filled the pages of Mother's Sears and Roebuck catalog (hats, chaps, boots, toy six-guns, thirty-two different designs of belt buckles, and the first of the children's school lunch boxes). His fan mail, ofttimes addressed simply to "Roy Rogers, King of the Cowboys," found its way to Republic Studios without the slightest delay.

We Buckaroos, as he was fond of calling us, joined Roy

Rogers Fan Clubs, bought twenty-eight million Roy Rogers comic books a year, and prompted publishers to produce no fewer than nineteen hardback books based on his fictional heroics. We listened to him sing and yodel on old RCA Victor 78s and devotedly read a syndicated newspaper comic strip which reached sixty-three million readers weekly. His weekly statement for his radio sponsor, "I was raised on Quaker Oats," made us want to eat Quaker Oats ourselves. And we stood ever ready to argue with the greatest conviction that our hero could ride, shoot, fight, and sing better than all the other box office cowboys you could crowd onto a movie screen.

It was a period in American life when heroics were in bountiful supply. Yet in my adolescent fantasy world there were none to compare with the silver-screen derring-do of Roy Rogers as he exposed mortgage-foreclosing bankers for the wicked men they were, rounded up scruffy bands of dastardly cattle rustlers, rescued damsels from all manner of distress, and generally championed countless underdogs trying to tame the West.

As I gained a touch of worldliness, I even came to see what Roy saw in Dale Evans. Not only was she smart, pretty, and able to ride a horse with the best of them, but she had that familiar Texas ring to her voice that would have made her a welcomed visitor in our home even if Roy had been detained at the studio.

Such was the stuff of which Saturday-afternoon heroes (and, yes, heroines) were once made. It was a different time in movie history, a time when one need not consult some alphabetic rating to be sure that Roll On Texas Moon or Under Western Stars or Along the Navajo Trail was fit entertainment for the kids. It was a time when good was good and bad was bad and the twain ne'er met.

To say that I was hesitant when asked to help in the writing of the book now in your hands would be a gross violation of truth in packaging. It was, on the other hand, a project not undertaken without considerable thought. I had never before done a book whose central characters I would, under different circumstances, have probably asked for autographs (no doubt lying that they were for my children). Which is to say that the opportunity to work with people I have admired for a great portion of my life, people who were and are a vital part of Americana, is equal parts humbling and challenging.

Except for an occasional paragraph here and there, the words are those of Roy and Dale. This aging, bearded Buckaroo simply served as the middleman, and therefore was spared many of the journalistic pitfalls of putting in too much color, or of dwelling too long on the movie make-believe Roy and Dale and missing the best part—the real-life people.

But if I may be allowed a final personal observation before getting on with the story, let me say that the Roy Rogers and Dale Evans I've come to know—the husband and wife with abounding talent, the mother and father with rock-strong convictions about their God and their country—are even more courageous than those I first met back on those bygone Saturday afternoons.

—CARLTON STOWERS

Preface

THE VIEW FROM THE UPSTAIRS BALCONY of the Roy Rogers–
Dale Evans Museum is, to my way of thinking, one of the
most beautiful scenes one is likely to find anywhere. Watching
the morning sun slide over the mountains, seeing the tumbleweeds lazily rolling along the wide-open, still-free High Desert
country of California, smelling the clean, smog-free air is about
as close to the Great Reward as I ever expect to get in this life.

Standing there, waiting for the coffee to come to a boil, it
finally occurred to me that it wasn't really such a bad idea. It
might even be fun—and it is certainly a testimony to the fact
that wonders, large and small, never cease.

Roy Rogers, the man who never walked across the stage
to receive a high school diploma and a handshake, writing a
book? It has been my good fortune in life to have done a
number of things, but rest assured this isn't one I ever even
dreamed of trying—not until the people at Word Books suggested the idea. Even then it sounded a little far-fetched to
me. Our life story has, to my way of thinking, been told to a
fare-thee-well by newspaper reporters, magazine journalists, and
my own favorite writer, Dale Evans. More about her later.

But Floyd Thatcher at Word Books was gently persuasive.
Yes, he agreed, there had already been a great deal printed
about Dale's and my life. Sure, there were a lot of stories
that might have a familiar ring to the people who had read
about us before. But, he pointed out, they will never have
read them as written by Roy Rogers.

15

So, call it vanity if you like. Challenging is probably a better word. He had struck a nerve. It was something to think about. And the more I thought about it, the more it occurred to me that there *are* some things I would like to say. And, as a fully-confessed sentimental slob, I have to admit great pleasure in the remembering. Which isn't to say all the trails have been happy. There have been a few sad songs along the way. There have been good times and bad, pain and sorrow—right along with the happiness and the rewards. Nothing unique about that, really. That's the way life is; that's what living is all about.

And that's what this book is about.

It occurs to me that I can tell you what this book *isn't* much easier than I can tell you what it *is*. It isn't two members of the entertainment world sitting down to recreate the plots of all their old movies, relive a few glories, salute a few directors and fellow actors, admit to the thrill of being in show business, and be done with it. Neither is it a sermon. There is name-dropping only because the names happen to be those of people who played vital and important parts in our lives.

After a lot of discussion, Dale and I decided that if we were going to coauthor the story of our lives, it would not be one aimed point-blank at the nostalgia craze which seems to be sweeping the country at present. Certainly the entertainment business has been a big part of our lives and livelihood, but it is by no means the Alpha and Omega. Aside from the fact that there was a time when we appeared on the screen about twenty times bigger than life and always did the bad guy in and came to a happy and just ending after approximately ninety minutes of running time, we are really no different from a lot of other husbands and wives throughout the country who will never be asked to write their life story. This is as much the story of Leonard Slye and Frances Octavia Smith (our original names) as it is of Roy Rogers, King of the Cowboys, and Dale Evans, Queen of the West.

It is the story of a family which, for reasons I'll probably never totally understand, had the good fortune to have been adopted, in a manner of speaking, by millions of people who were interested in who we are and what we do.

It is a very personal story—more personal, in fact, than I

had planned it to be. But as I committed myself to the project
I became increasingly aware of the need for it to have a strong
ring of truth. Dale settled that issue before the first piece of
blank paper went into the typewriter. "They're not asking you
to win the Pulitzer Prize," she told me, "just tell an honest
story."

It is, of course, a story which, even if I were properly gifted,
I couldn't tell alone. It is not only my story. Thus the lady of
the house has agreed to take an equal turn at the wheel. Like
I told her, marriage and book-writing are fifty-fifty propositions.

I do, however, want to make it clear that I am not entering
the field of writing completely without journalistic background.
First, Dale, whose shoulder I've not only been leaning on but
looking over for thirty-one years, has distinguished herself with
enough best-selling books to line an entire shelf in my den.
I've read them all. It seems reasonable to assume that some
of that has rubbed off somewhere along the line.

And it was I, if you'll remember, who played the part of a
crusading country editor in *Home in Oklahoma* back in 1946.
Not exactly the same way Ernest Hemingway got his start,
I'll admit, but, the way I look at it, you pick up your pointers
where you find them.

So let's get on with it.

—Roy Rogers

Part One

*King of
the Cowboys*

*H*E STOOD in the sparse shade of an ancient Texas mesquite wearing jeans, boots, and a straw Western hat, looking neither his age—sixty-three years —nor, for that matter, like the American legend he had become. His one hundred seventy-pound frame was that of an active man; there remained the familiar slight squint of the eyes, the rich baritone voice, the slightly bowed legs, and the disarming smile.

There, under a brain-baking Texas sun, on location at the 6666 Ranch, the King of the Cowboys was again making a movie after a twenty-year absence. For the constant stream of reporters who came to the sprawling cattle ranch outside the tiny Texas Panhandle hamlet of Guthrie, and for the daily visitors from surrounding communities, nostalgia had come to life. Roy Rogers was back, and they had all come to share in the welcome.

Even the cast and crew of Mackintosh and T. J. felt they were a part of something special. Veteran stuntman and actor Dean Smith, who was playing a ranch hand in this contemporary Western written especially with Roy Rogers in mind, said, "You know, when I was a kid growing up here in Texas I can remember keeping this scrapbook on Roy. I'd cut all his pictures out of the newspapers and magazines. He was the man I wanted to grow up to be. It's a great thrill for me just to be working on a movie with him."

He smiled, glancing over to where Roy stood talking with his fourteen-year-old co-star Clay O'Brien. "That boy," Smith said, "probably has no idea what an opportunity this is for him. Back in my day there were several million of us who

21

would have gladly committed high crimes to be standing in that youngster's shoes."

Guich Kooch, another Texan who would soon establish himself as a television star with his role in the popular "Carter Country" series, also made no attempt to mask his enthusiasm. "Frankly," he noted, "I'm not all that crazy about the movie business, but when I heard they were planning to shoot this one with Roy Rogers, I caught the first plane out to California and let everyone know I had to be in it. I know Roy thinks I'm crazy, but the first thing I did when I got here was ask him for an autographed picture."

All of which Roy Rogers found amusing. "Sure," he told a collection of reporters dispatched by editors to chronicle his return to the motion picture business, "it's been fun being a hero to so many kids over the years. And I like to think that what we did was a positive kind of thing—something a little worthwhile. The movie business has been mighty good to me."

And he to it. For an Ohio farm kid whose greatest ambition in life was to one day be a doctor, the idea of being an actor began as a lark, later developed into a possible method of assuring himself and his new bride three meals a day, and finally became a way of life.

The medical profession's loss was the gain of Saturday's children throughout the world.

1

You'll FORGIVE MY IMMODESTY if I point to the fact that each spring something in the neighborhood of a million people—men, women and children of all ages—visit my birthplace. But, in all honesty, not for the reason you might think.

The address of the old home place was 412 Second Street, Cincinnati, Ohio. It was, I'm told, a red brick tenement building whose best features were the facts that the roof didn't leak unless it really came a downpour and that it was in close proximity to my father's job at the United States Shoe Company.

The building is no longer there. For that matter, neither is the four-hundred block of Second Street. Urban Renewal saw to that some years back. In its place the city fathers elected to have Riverfront Stadium built to serve as the home of the major league Cincinnati Reds.

And as best I can determine, the place I was born was roughly where second base is now located. So, in reality, it isn't the birthplace of Roy Rogers those million people I mentioned come to see but, rather, the double plays turned by the hometown infield. Which is quite as it should be. Still, how many people do you know who can say they were born at second base in a big league ball park? It's not a bad yarn to spin to your grandkids, you'll have to admit.

As a matter of fact, had one of my early boyhood aspirations materialized, I just might have made one of those triumphant returns to the old home place, not as a singing cowboy or, for that matter, as a second baseman, but as a big league

23

pitcher. Though my grade school teacher and coach, a man of rare athletic and academic abilities named Guy Baumgartner, probably doesn't remember it exactly the way I do, my curve ball was once the terror of the schoolground. (Granted, it has curved better and with greater velocity with the passage of time, but then that's the privilege of aging athletes, right?)

Still, when you get right down to it, my abilities as a baseball player never caused a single major league scout to come running to our doorstep with promises of fame and fortune. No big league pitcher ever lost any sleep worrying about having his job stolen away by a skinny right-hander named Leonard Slye.

But it didn't hurt to dream. My father taught me that.

Andy Slye was a small, easygoing man of incredible energy, a man with a creative knack for building everything and repairing almost anything. He loved life, music, the out-of-doors, my mother, and each of his children. And he was a bit of a dreamer, a romantic, an adventurer. I used to love to sit and hear him tell stories about his younger days, before he met and married Mom, when he followed the whims of youth from one marvelous adventure to another.

As a teenager, he once traveled across the country with a carnival as a laborer, and later performed as an acrobat for a while. A self-taught musician, he once worked as an entertainer on a showboat and was a big hit with his guitar and mandolin at square dances throughout Ohio. He used to tell about sitting on the wharves of Portsmouth for hours on end, watching ships from magical, far-away places as they unloaded their cargoes. He would make up fantasies about the ships and their crews, fashioning exciting stories in his mind. From that fertile imagination would later come the stories he would tell my sisters and me.

Dad never said as much, but I've always felt that the only thing in the world that could have made him give up his wandering and adventure-seeking was his love for my mother. She was working in a laundry when Dad first met her and began asking her out on dates. A couple of years older than he was, she made it clear to him that she would never consider marrying a man who was not ready to settle down, hold a job, and devote himself to raising a family.

Which is not to say Mattie Slye didn't like her fun, too. Born in Kentucky, she also had a deep-seated love for music. She played a variety of string instruments and, despite having been crippled by polio as a baby, loved to go to dances.

I should also point out that Mom's marriage to Dad didn't exactly shake all the wanderlust from his shoes. . . .

SHORTLY AFTER THE BIRTH OF HIS SON, Andy Slye began plotting to escape the bustle and confinement of Cincinnati. His job in the lasting department at the shoe company had become akin to a prison sentence. The outdoors beckoned him, travel whispered in his ear, adventure called. So he enlisted the help of his blind brother Will in constructing a houseboat from lumber salvaged from a wrecked steamboat.

Friends good-naturedly referred to it as Andy's Ark. Andy Slye called it his family's ticket to a better, more carefree life. In July of 1912 they boarded their newly-whitewashed, twelve-by-fifty-foot, three-room home and floated off down the Ohio River toward Portsmouth. It would be a journey the Swiss Family Robinson would have appreciated.

The first day out a sudden summer storm ripped to shreds the boat's sail, which had been fashioned from a half-dozen of Mattie Slye's best bedsheets. The mast was hurled into the river as the houseboat pitched on the storm-chopped river. Inside the cabin Andy Slye tried to comfort his family, all the while privately questioning the soundness of his plan, which just hours earlier had been one of great promise and excitement.

But aside from the loss of Mattie's bedsheets, a broken dish here and there, and an untimely collision with a stray raft (which caused only minimal damage to the floating Slye home), the storm would be remembered as little more than an exciting episode in a great adventure.

Along the way Andy worked at odd jobs, anchoring long enough to set nets for fishing boats in return for a tow on down the river. The journey would finally end with the docking near a landing in Portsmouth. And for the next four years of his life, the man who was destined to one day become King

of the Cowboys spent more time on the water than he did
on land.

It is understandable that he remembers little of those times;
the family gatherings on deck on summer evenings for sing-
alongs, the picnics shared beneath the shade of dogwood trees
and clusters of pawpaw bushes, the swimming and fishing.

For instance, Roy doesn't recall the day his mother happened
on him as he stood near the protective railing, systematically
and with great joy tossing the family silverware into the river,
delighting at the plunking sound each piece made as it hit
the water and then sank. (Mattie Slye retrieved all her silverware
when the river went down.)

Nor does he own firsthand knowledge of the great Portsmouth flood which set the Slye houseboat afloat and sent land-
locked homes washing away from their foundations. During
the thirteen days of the flood, Andy Slye skillfully poled his
houseboat through the streets of Portsmouth, rescuing people
stranded on rooftops or floating along on pieces of torn-away
debris. Before the water receded, Andy's Ark had finally lived
up to its name; it was filled to overflowing with homeless victims,
stray dogs, and an odd assortment of personal belonging which
had been saved.

The flood, for all the misery and destruction it caused, provided the Slyes with a rare opportunity to relocate. Mary, the
eldest of the Slye daughters, was nearing school age, and Mattie
was expecting her fourth child soon. It had been agreed that
the luxury of life on the river would have to be set aside in
favor of a more populated area where schools and doctors
were closer at hand. Andy, in fact, had already purchased a
lot in Portsmouth where he planned to build a home. Instead,
however, he simply navigated the houseboat to the proper spot
on Mill Street and let it settle into place—instant house.

The final chapter in another adventure story written, Andy
Slye again found himself working in a shoe factory while his
family adjusted themselves once again to life in the city.

It was a change of lifestyle born more of necessity than desire.
Neither Andy nor his young son was able to forsake the life
of freedom and open spaces completely. The rewards of punching a clock at the shoe factory were basic to Andy—a regular

paycheck kept groceries in Mattie's cupboards and proper clothes on the backs of his children. Beyond that it was uninspiring drudgery, hardly satisfying to a man whose soul was that of half dreamer, half adventurer.

For young Leonard the paved streets of the city failed to provide many of the delightful mysteries which had surrounded him as he grew up on the river. With no squirrels to chase, no raccoons to track or rabbits to hunt, he turned his attention to more domestic animals. The Slye home became the way station for a constant parade of stray and hungry dogs and cats, but his Samaritan inclinations were not restricted to animals. Once he arrived in Mattie's kitchen leading a sick and elderly man he had found suffering from amnesia. On another occasion it was a young child—scared, lost, and hungry.

Leonard's compassion, his concern for the physical welfare of virtually all of God's creatures, would form the foundation of his greatest ambition. Young Leonard began to make it clear to anyone interested enough to listen that he would one day become a doctor. There are those who knew him as a youngster who feel the ambition was born from his constant concern for the human miseries he saw daily. There was his beloved mother, with her crippled leg, and his blind Uncle Will. Leonard felt their suffering, and in his youthful fantasies saw himself one day helping people like them.

Until such time that he was qualified to undertake such healings, however, he would content himself with mending the homeless animals he brought regularly to the house on Mill Street.

"I don't think anyone really realized how serious he had become about being a doctor," Andy Slye once told a reporter, "until his little ol' mongrel puppy got its leg broken. With his mother's help he put a splint on the dog's leg, fixed it a bed from an old quilt, fed it warm milk, and spent every spare minute he had pouring love and attention on that little dog."

Finally the time came when his parents agreed the splint had been on long enough for the bone to heal. With great care and obvious excitement, Leonard removed the wrappings. Once free of the splint, the dog slowly stepped from the youngster's lap and began to walk across the kitchen floor. Leonard's *face froze in disappointment; tears came to his eyes. The dog put no weight on the crippled leg. The bone had mended, but in such a way that it made the leg useless.*

The failure sank his spirit, but at the same time reinforced his determination to become a doctor. It served to make it clearer to him that reaching his goal was going to be difficult. "But I'm going to do it," he told his mother, who had tried to console him by pointing out that his care and attention had no doubt saved the little dog's life, even if it hadn't made its leg like new. "I want to be able to fix things right," he argued. Mattie Slye smiled, nodded, and hugged her young son.

As time passed, Andy Slye became more and more convinced that the city was not the proper environment for children. It was a subject he and his wife had spoken of often, but the discussions came more frequently and grew more serious following a call one evening from the police. Leonard and one of his neighborhood friends had hopped a ride on an ice wagon and, once discovered by the angry driver, had been taken to the police station. Both were frightened and crying when their parents came to get them and assured them that their crime was not of such magnitude to merit being locked away.

The incident, however, lent fire to Andy Slye's desire to get his family out of the city and back to the country life. He had been able to save a little money, and had even managed to purchase a second-hand Maxwell touring car.

Money and transportation were the two things he needed to be able to embark on his next adventure. Thus in 1919, when Leonard was eight, Andy purchased a small farm in the rolling brush country on Duck Run, twelve miles outside Portsmouth. With the help of relatives and his children, he built a six-room farmhouse which would replace the houseboat as the Slye residence. It lacked indoor plumbing and had no electricity, but it had plenty of coal-oil lamps. It was really a home.

THE FIRST THING I LEARNED about life on the farm was that no matter if the sun was boiling hot or there was rain coming down in sheets or it was below freezing with snow knee deep, a cow was still a cow and had to be fed and milked. And that chickens still laid eggs and needed their nests cleaned, and that hogs still needed to be slopped.

And I believe to this day that the wood box we kept in the kitchen must have had a hole in the bottom of it. One of my chores was to see that it stayed full, and it seemed forever empty despite my efforts.

My efforts, you should understand, weren't more than a drop in the bucket compared to those of my father. He cleared land, burned stumps and pulled them out with a mule; he built a barn for the milk cows, pens for the hogs; he planted and plowed, and somehow still had energy left after dinner for music. But he knew that it would be close to impossible for us to make it on the farm alone, so he went back to work at the shoe factory as soon as he had set everything in order in Duck Run.

That, I think, was probably the hardest thing he ever had to do. In those days twelve miles was a long trip. So he was forced to stay in Portsmouth during the week, coming home to the farm on the weekends. It was lonely and hard for him— and for us as well—but it was the only way he could see to provide us with the environment he felt was so important to his children.

Like every other farm family I've known, we worked hard and, when the opportunity afforded itself, played hard. It was my responsibility to tend the animals, fill the woodbox, and do the plowing. Admittedly, these weren't the greatest forms of recreation in the world, but there was always the knowledge that, once completed, there were things like fishing and swimming in the nearby creek, hikes into the Ohio hills, picnics on warm summer days, and more wild animals than you could shake a stick at. It sure beat chasing the ice wagon back on Mill Street.

I had pet skunks, a groundhog, a couple of raccoons, more dogs than I can even remember, and a rooster that I trained to sit on my shoulder. If times were hard in those days—which certainly they were—the fact usually escaped my notice.

Dad got paid every two weeks, and he would always come home with presents for everyone. There was one he brought me which I'll never forget; the afternoon he came home with

Babe, a black mare who in her earlier life had been a sulky racer, still has to rank as one of the most memorable of my life. Never mind that she dumped me right on the seat of my britches the first time I got on her. It was love at first sight as far as I was concerned. I just dusted off my pants, stroked her mane a little and talked with her and climbed back on.

She was quick to pick up a few simple tricks I began to teach her as soon as we got acquainted. I thought she was, without question, the most beautiful and the smartest animal the good Lord had ever created. Of course, the only first-hand comparison I could make at the time was with an ornery old plow mule with whom I had had a running feud from the time we moved to the farm.

As I grew older and satisfied Mom that I was a qualified horseman, I was occasionally allowed to ride Babe into Portsmouth and pay a visit to Dad on weekends when he couldn't get home. When the budget allowed, he would treat me to a movie.

Years later, I mentioned those trips to the movies to a reporter, adding that my favorite star was Hoot Gibson. Shortly after that, a story appeared, saying that while sitting there in that little Portsmouth picture show I made up my mind that I was going to grow up to be the "King of the Cowboys."

Which is nothing more than a Grade-A pasteurized Hollywood publicity story. The truth of the matter was that the only things that seemed really important to me at that time were being able to eat all I wanted and sleeping as late as I could in the mornings (but the cow always had to be milked). And, in the back of my mind, there was that dream of being a doctor. Elbowing in on Hoot Gibson's terrain never came to mind.

For an aspiring young Doctor Kildare, I'm afraid I wasn't exactly an academic whiz. School, as a matter of fact, became more and more of a problem as I went from one grade to the next.

With Dad working in Portsmouth, the job of running the farm demanded a great deal of my time before I went off to school and was waiting for me when I returned. If we had

had a dollar for every night I fell asleep at the kitchen table, trying to study by the light of a kerosene lamp, we would have been able to hire help and probably buy a second-hand tractor.

The fact that my grades did not reflect the same scholarly abilities as some of my classmates worried me. No, worried isn't the proper word. It embarrassed me. And I handled it about as poorly as it could be handled. To draw attention from my poor performances in the classroom, I became the class show-off, a blue-ribbon smart aleck who did his dead-level best to be sure the teacher earned his money.

One morning one of my classmates was on the receiving end of what I felt was a little too severe whipping, and I jumped up and came to his defense. What resulted was a good country whipping for me as well, and something close to mutiny in the little one-room schoolhouse.

Things didn't get much better as time passed. Once I threw a girl's cap up on the roof of the school (after she had thrown mine up there). The teacher, having witnessed my mischief, demanded that I climb up and get it. I said, "Not until she gets mine," and the teacher dashed off in search of the paddle.

The chase was on. I finally ran into a shallow creek, certain the teacher wouldn't follow, and panicked when I quickly saw that was not to be the case. I picked up a rock and threw it at my pursuer, hitting him in the forehead. Scared and ashamed of what I had done, I then ran home.

The term juvenile delinquent had not become a part of the nation's vocabulary when I was in the sixth grade, but, looking back, I shudder to think of the direction I was headed.

A man named Guy Baumgartner arrived just in time. The former teacher, having all he wanted of Duck Run—and, no doubt, of Leonard Slye—resigned at the end of the school year. In his place came a middle-aged man who had a constant smile fixed on his face, a gift for making education fun, and the patience and ability to make me aware of the importance of learning. He even insisted that all the students call him Guy rather than Mr. Baumgartner.

I've never fully understood how it is God knows when and whom to bring into your life, but his timing was perfect in this case. Over the years it has been my good fortune to have a lot of wonderful people play a part in my life. None ever did so in a more positive manner than that schoolteacher back in Duck Run.

To him the learning process included more than books and blackboards and homework. He organized athletic teams, led us on nature hikes, and established a 4-H program, urging those of us who could to purchase a baby pig and try to raise a prizewinner.

For ten dollars, I became the proud owner of a newborn black Poland China pig which, with a little suggesting from my sisters, I named Evangeline. She grew up to be the grand champion at the Scioto County Fair held in Lucasville, and earned me a trip to visit the state capitol, Columbus, Ohio.

It was Guy Baumgartner, I suppose, who gave me my first acting job—if you want to call playing Santa Claus in the school Christmas play a first step toward B-Western stardom. I can say without reservation that I never made a movie or did a television show or performed on a stage that terrified me as much as standing there in front of a couple of dozen people at the Duck Run School, trying to "ho-ho-ho," thinking I was going to die of sheer agony.

I don't think I'd have even considered doing it for anyone but Guy Baumgartner. I owed him. For that matter, I still do.

No matter how hard we worked at it, the demands of making a go of it on the farm seemed always a step ahead of us. Oh, there were fun times, and a sense of freedom that only that kind of lifestyle can provide. But, looking at it from a cold, businesslike point of view, it seemed at times like we were trying to dig a hole in the sand. Dad, trying to divide his time between the shoe factory and the farm, would get discouraged, and the feeling would sweep through the family—to Mom, to me, and to the girls.

Since the Duck Run school had only eight grades, I was enrolled in a high school at McDermott, Ohio, about four miles from Duck Run, for my freshman and sophomore years.

I was pretty good at sports, not bad at the clarinet, okay with my studies, and a galloping failure with the girls. There

was this pretty auburn-haired trumpet player in the school orchestra with whom I fell madly in love and whom, after several
weeks of practice and nerve-building, I finally asked to be my
date at a band recital. I had every intention of sweeping her
off her feet with clever and witty conversation.

This, to the best of my recollection, was how the conversation
went that evening: After I picked her up she made the observation that it was most certainly a warm evening, wasn't it? I
dazzled her with my reply: "Yes, it certainly is." Later, the
recital over, I took her home and she said, "It's a bit cooler
now, isn't it?" "Yes, it is," I said.

I decided to postpone romance and work on baseball.

Which was just as well, really, since the time was nearing
for the family to make another move—back to Cincinnati.

I was seventeen then, and felt it time for me to help Dad
carry the load of financial responsibility. Despite my mother's
reservations—she had been openly concerned about the possibility of my dropping out of school in the early days in Duck
Run—I quit school and went to work alongside Dad in the
shoe factory in Cincinnati. The thirty-five dollars a week they
would pay me, it had finally been agreed, would help with
the family finances and still leave enough to pay for night
school.

For a while it worked. I would get off at the shoe factory,
have dinner, and go off to night classes which lasted from
eight to eleven-thirty. As time went on, however, it became
harder and harder to find time to get homework assignments
completed on time. Tired from the routine of working by day
and going to school at night, I wasn't exactly setting any records
for retention either.

One evening, in the middle of class, I decided to rest my
head on the desk for a minute during a lecture. I did not
awake until a fellow sitting next to me poked me in the ribs
to tell me that class was just about over.

Several of the students got a good laugh out of the incident.
But it would be their last at Leonard Slye's expense. Someone
else would have to grow up to heal the sick and the afflicted.
I had come to the realization that the task would not fall to

me. Embarrassed by my untimely catnap and weary of chasing academic rainbows, I gave it up. I never went back to school.

WORKING FULL-TIME at the shoe factory, I soon came to appreciate the drudgery my father had so long endured. Weeks seemed to stretch endlessly until finally it would be Friday and I could look forward to a weekend of freedom. As often as possible I would return to the farm where my sister Cleda and her new husband were living. It was good to be back in the open spaces, to work out-of-doors by day and go hunting at night. But there would always be a new week and time to clock in again at the factory.

On one particular Monday morning, as I made my way about the house, getting ready for work as if I were locked into slow motion, I looked in on Dad to see if he was about ready. I found him still in bed; Mom was pressing a damp cloth to his forehead. "Your father," she told me, "isn't going to work today. He's got a horrible headache."

I stood there in the doorway for a moment, looking down on my father, saying nothing. I couldn't remember his having had a headache before. Suddenly I was fully awake, no longer in slow motion. In fact, there were several things running through my mind at once. I thought of the letters from my sister Mary, who had married and moved to California. And of the fact that our jobs at the shoe factory were roads leading nowhere.

"Dad," I finally said, "I've got something over ninety dollars saved up. You ought to have right at a hundred. What do you say we just up and quit our jobs, go out to visit Mary, and take a look at California? She says the country's beautiful, and it seems to me there's likely jobs to be had out there."

You never saw a headache go away so fast. Suddenly Dad was sitting up in bed, talking with great enthusiasm about my proposal.

Mom, bless her, took the damp cloth away and left the room, silently shaking her head. Now, she was no doubt thinking, she had *two* daydreaming adventurers on her hands.

She started packing that day. We loaded our 1923 Dodge and started the long drive west.

The old Dodge didn't make it, but we did. We got as far as Magdelina, New Mexico, before the bearings burned out; we fixed them from parts of another old Dodge in a junkyard and continued on to California. Fixing the car shot quite a hole in our vacation budget. Suffice it to say, then, that we didn't exactly arrive at Mary's home in Lawndale putting on any airs, packed as we were into an aging jalopy that badly needed a paint job and did far more shaking and rattling than it did rolling.

But aside from being broke, hungry, and bone-weary, we were just fine. A few days' rest took care of the weariness, Mary's abilities in the kitchen chased the hunger, and her husband did his part to solve our financial problems by giving us jobs driving gravel trucks for him.

We stayed four months before heading back for Ohio. None of us were too anxious to leave, but Dad insisted it was time. "Maybe," he said, "I'll just see about putting the farm up for sale when we get back and we'll move out here for good. I'm not a half-bad truck driver, and it sure beats being cooped up in a shoe factory."

Patience not being one of my long suits at the time, I was hardly home before I found myself headed back to California. Mary's father-in-law was going there, so I suggested going along to help him with the driving. The following spring, the rest of the family followed, and the old farm shifted to the shoulders of some of our neighbors, the Hiles family, who still own it.

Dad rented a little house near where Mary and her husband were living, and before Mom could even get curtains hung he and I had jobs driving trucks for a road construction operation. We regularly took turns applauding our foresightedness in making the move west—until the morning we reported for work just in time to see all the trucks being towed away. Our employer had gone bankrupt, and quite suddenly bountiful California began to look a great deal like hard-times Ohio.

2

It was spring of 1930 when the Andy Slye family, like so many preceding them, loaded their most essential belongings into their 1923 Dodge and pointed it in the direction of California, chasing once again the promise of a better life.

The constant battle of two-dollar woes and the slim prospect of a more prosperous future were the journey's chief motivating factors. The Great Depression was casting its clouded pall over the country, and the Slyes were no different from the literally thousands of Americans who looked toward California as the place where their hard luck would change.

Years later, financial hard times well behind him, Roy Rogers would read The Grapes of Wrath, *John Steinbeck's moving account of Dust Bowl refugees migrating west in hope of a better tomorrow, and would marvel at its accuracy. "There are parts in that book," Roy says, "that made me wonder if maybe Mr. Steinbeck wasn't looking over the shoulders of the Slye family."*

He, his father, and his cousin Stanley Slye, after a succession of short-lived jobs, joined the legions of new arrivals traveling from one orchard to another, picking fruit for low and often irregular wages. They would work long hours, their day's service ending only with the welcome arrival of darkness. Then they would climb into their pickup and travel in the direction of the next orchard in need of harvesting. Makeshift campsites along the way became a familiar sight, and impromptu communities would spring to life in the clearings off the highways.

"Food was about the only thing more scarce than money," he remembers, *"so we ate a lot of fruit. But after a while you get to a point where you figure if you have to eat another peach or handful of grapes you'd just as soon starve to death. So I made me a slingshot and every once in a while got lucky hunting rabbits."*

One evening the wearied Slye clan sat around their campfire, glad that their day in the orchards was behind them, and all but hypnotized by the aroma of the coffee and frying rabbit. They were anxiously anticipating their first meal of the day.

"All at once," Roy remembers, *"there were several little kids standing around, sad-faced and wearing about the worst-looking clothes you ever saw. A couple of mangy-looking dogs that were with them stood, just looking, every bit as silent as their little masters. Nobody said anything; they just stood there, looking over at that frying pan.*

"It wasn't too hard to read their minds."

Thus on that particular evening the Slye's meal was limited to cups of the coffee Andy had brewed. The fried rabbit, cut into as many portions as possible, was quickly and enthusiastically consumed by the youthful visitors to the campsite.

Afterwards, spirits lifted as stomachs welcomed a new warmth. The youngsters stayed to talk and listen as their hosts entertained with music. Leonard Slye strummed his guitar and sang while Andy and Stanley played their mandolins and provided harmony.

In time, nightly sing-songs would be a familiar occurrence for those migrant workers who stayed the night near the Slye camping spot. On occasion there would even be enough energy left for members of the movable population to enjoy a square dance under the California stars. Never much of a dancer, Leonard Slye would generally serve as caller.

It was music, then, which would briefly relieve the Slyes and their evening visitors of the burdens they had carried through the day. The music brought smiles to faces which seldom had other occasion to smile; it cheered the cheerless and replaced bone-wearing drudgery with a few hours of fun.

It was on those long ago evenings that young Leonard Slye,

*still seeking the proper direction for his life, first really recog-
nized the importance and purpose of music. Up to that time
it had been little more than a joyfully accepted but taken-for-
granted part of his life. In the Slye home, he will admit today,
there were occasions when material goods were in short supply.
There was, however, always plenty of happiness and music.*

AFTER A COUPLE OF MONTHS of nonproductive job hunting and
almost nonpaying fruitpicking, Dad got word that a Los Angeles
shoe company was hiring. There was a resignation in his eyes
that I'll never forget. He didn't say as much, but I knew how
he hated the idea of returning to that line of work. "A man
takes what's available to him, son," he told me. "You coming
along?"

A long silence passed between us. It answered him better
than I was able to. "Dad," I said, "the only thing that I really
have an honest good feeling for is music. It makes me happy,
and my playing and singing seems to make everyone else
happy. If I can talk cousin Stanley into it, I'd like to take a
try at being a musician. From what I hear, there are always
a lot of social meetings and parties and square dances to play
at. Some of the better groups are even working on the radio
a lot.

"I'd be crazy to say that I know how it'll work out," I continued, "but I'll never know until I give it a try."

Looking back on it now, I can see that there probably isn't
a person in the world who better understood what I felt, what
I was trying to say, than Andy Slye. What he realized, I suppose,
is that more than a little of himself had rubbed off on his
son. He wished me well and went to the shoe factory alone.

I'LL NOT ASK for a show of hands of those of you who remember
a couple of skinny hillbilly-looking singers who called themselves The Slye Brothers. Their debut caused not a ripple.
Their earning power was limited to depending on the generosity
of square dancers and partygoers who saw fit to drop a little
something in the hat as it was passed. We never had any trouble
lifting the hat after it had made the rounds.

Leonard and Stanley Slye were, to put it mildly, several

light years away from being household names in the West Coast music business.

There were times, though, when it looked as if we were on our way. One night, after hearing us play at a square dance, this fellow who identified himself as an agent said a lot of nice things about the way we were singing. He suggested we get together for a cup of coffee after the dance. Before you knew it, he was talking about booking us into some theaters, maybe even working up some kind of tour.

The few places we did work weren't exactly the Hollywood Bowl and, as it was explained to us, the money we were earning was somehow being eaten up by expenses. Pretty soon the "agent" disappeared, and the not-so-famous and not-so-smart Slye Brothers were back to passing the hat.

"Len," Stanley finally said one day, "we've got to talk. Let's go get a piece of pie." I had this old motorcycle then, and we rode all the way into downtown Los Angeles to this place where you could get half a pie for a dime.

"We're getting nowhere fast," Stanley said—something of an understatement. "I'm ready to call it quits and see if I can find a job that has a paycheck to go with it. Besides, if I stick with it we're liable to run across that 'agent' of ours somewhere along the line, and I'm afraid they might put me in jail for what I would do to him."

"Being the kind of fella he obviously is," I said, "we'd probably have to stand in a long line just to get our chance."

We laughed, finished our pie, and with no great fanfare or additional speeches abolished The Slye Brothers. I went in search of the next step in my own limping musical career.

Trying to somehow convince myself that experience was almost as valuable as money, I played a while for a group called Uncle Tom Murray's Hollywood Hillbillies. Uncle Tom also placed high value on experience, and therefore never felt a need to offer me any kind of salary for my contribution.

A small radio station in Inglewood announced that it planned to conduct an amateur singing contest, and Mom and Mary urged me to enter. I decided I might as well, inasmuch as I was about as close to an amateur singer as they were likely to find anywhere.

As the date of the contest neared, everyone in the family got very excited about attending to serve as my personal cheering section. The more excited they got, the more nervous I got. When the big night finally arrived, I would have gladly traded the guitar I had bought back in Ohio for a spot on the assembly line down at the shoe factory. Singing with Stanley at dances and small parties or joining into the harmony with The Hollywood Hillbillies had been one thing; going up on a stage to compete against a bunch of other singers, each of whom I was thoroughly convinced was far better than I, was something else entirely.

When my name was called I froze to my chair. Mary nudged me with an elbow a couple of times, gently at first and then with a little more enthusiasm. "Len," she finally said, making no attempt at masking her rising anger, "we've come all the way down here to hear you sing. I sewed that fancy shirt for you and Mama ironed your pants. So get up right now and go up there and show them how good you can play and sing."

It was useless to try to explain to her that if my legs wouldn't work—which they suddenly didn't seem to want to do—there certainly was no reason to believe my vocal cords were going to behave any better.

I'll skip the O. Henry ending to this little tale by simply stating that I did not win. I didn't even place. The truth is, the only real applause for my efforts came from the row of seats occupied by members of the immediate Slye family.

The following day, however, I got a call from a man who identified himself as the manager of a Western music group which called itself The Rocky Mountaineers. He said he had liked my singing and wanted to know if I was interested in joining his group. It had, he explained, a regular weekly program on a station in Long Beach and, while they received no pay for the show, they were allowed to use air time to plug the fact that they were available for parties and dances.

Not exactly swamped with offers at the moment, I jumped at the chance.

My association with the Mountaineers didn't exactly jump me into another tax bracket, but it did provide me with my first introduction to a couple of musicians who would later rank among the greatest that Western music has ever known.

Bob Nolan, an outstanding baritone who had just come to California from his native Canada and was a lifeguard at Santa Monica beach, joined the group shortly after I did, but left when he became aware that paydays were going to be few and far between. Though destined to become an outstanding songwriter, he took a job as a caddy at the Bel-Air Country Club. I've always wondered if he came up with the words and music to some of his outstanding compositions like "Tumbling Tumbleweeds" while hauling some golfer's bag around the plush, manicured Bel-Air course where, to be sure, never a tumbleweed tumbled.

Our advertisement for a baritone and yodeler to replace Nolan was answered by Tim Spencer, one of the thousands who had left Oklahoma's Dust Bowl in search of a more prosperous life in California. In the years to come that prosperity would be realized; Tim would write literally hundreds of Western tunes. Among my favorites were "Pioneer Mother of Mine," a song I still have trouble singing because it reminds me so of my mother, and "Roomful of Roses," which originally stayed on the Hit Parade for three months and is revived by someone every couple of years. In fact, just a couple of years ago, Mickey Gilley, the country-western singer, recorded it, and it immediately climbed to number one on the country-western charts.

Even with talent like that of Nolan and Spencer, however, it was hard going. One member of the group was married, and several of the others lived in a small house with him and his wife. The living room floor looked like a campground every night.

It was easy to see that an arrangement like that couldn't go on forever. And, sadly, it didn't. The time eventually came when people were dropping out faster than we could find replacements. The Rocky Mountaineers soon went the way of The Slye Brothers and The Hollywood Hillbillies.

But, to the everlasting credit of this crazy business, there's always another group waiting to be formed, certain that it will be the one to make it big. I was just too stubborn to give it up; Tim hadn't been at it long enough to be completely disenchanted; and Slumber Nichols, another holdover from the

Mountaineers, said he didn't have anything else to do but sing and go hungry. So we joined a group which called itself the International Cowboys and were soon back on the radio, singing for free. How's that for progress?

Enter another booking agent.

Resigned to the fact that a breakthrough for a new group was all but impossible in the Los Angeles area, where there seemed to be a bunch of guys singing Western music on every streetcorner, we talked about the possibility of trying a barnstorming tour, hitting the smaller towns in other states. The aforementioned agent, who to the best of my recollection was selling time on the radio station, said he would like to add a touch of refinement to our plan. He suggested a "Southwestern tour," taking our kind of show to a part of the world where good western music was properly appreciated—Arizona, New Mexico, and Texas. Once he knew that a member of the group had an automobile, he assured us he would set the dates for us and we could get on the road.

WHEN YOU'RE SINGING for free and have already accumulated a pretty sizable list of past failures, you understand, you grab at promises. Road map in hand, five of us from the International Cowboys hit the road to begin what has to be one of the most unsuccessful musical tours in entertainment history. Our new name, we decided, would be the O-Bar-O Cowboys.

Our first stop was Yuma, Arizona, where, despite the assurances of our "agent," not a single person in town had ever even heard of us, much less made preparations for a show. We never made a nickel in Yuma.

Next stop, Miami, Arizona. They were expecting us there, but not for another week. We were forced to take a week's vacation in Phoenix, which we needed like we needed four heads. We got on a radio station in Phoenix to advertise our appearance in Miami, which was a copper mining town.

But nobody bothered to tell us that the mines had long ago closed and that the town was just a few stubborn souls away from being officially a ghost town. We rode up and down main street with megaphones announcing our appearance that evening. Again, as in Yuma, we made no money; we were getting nowhere fast. We paid the bill at our tourist court with my wristwatch, just to get out of town.

There probably aren't a lot of people in the country who can tell you much about the little community of Safford, Arizona, but to this day it remains one of my favorite spots. It was there, after all our dead ends, that we found a paying job. Our performance netted us four dollars apiece, and to the man we were certain we had at last found the mother lode.

Our next stop seemed like a sure thing. Wilcox, Arizona was the hometown of one of the members of the group, so it stood to reason that this triumphant return would provide a sizable audience. Sure enough, when we got there, there were signs everywhere saying, "Welcome Home Cactus Mac." "Hometown Boy Makes Good in Hollywood," and generally proclaiming a hero's welcome.

We got our crowd all right, but the enthusiasm shown by the citizens of Wilcox caused our leader Cactus Mac to break out in a thundering case of homesickness. He announced to the group that he had thought about it and had decided to just stay there in Wilcox where he belonged and give up the music business. Our fiddle player owned the car and wanted to return to Los Angeles, so at three o'clock in the morning we had to talk him into going on to Roswell, New Mexico, which was our next booking.

It was in June of 1933 that we arrived in Roswell, short on money and again ahead of the schedule which had been set for us. We pooled our finances and came up with a grand total of two dollars. I got to thinking maybe we all should have stayed in Wilcox.

But when in a bind you make do. We talked the manager of a tourist court into extending us credit until after we were paid for our show, and went to the local radio station where the manager agreed to let us go on the air and sing a few songs to promote ourselves. He even loaned us a rifle so we could do some rabbit hunting, since it was unlikely that any of the grocery stores or restaurants were going to be interested in extending credit to a less than prosperous-looking group of musicians passing through.

We lived pretty well on cottontails and jack rabbits for quite a while. But even the rabbits became scarce in a week or so. One day all we could bag was a hawk, which we tried to boil on a hotplate in the room. We were hungry, and it tasted good, but suffice it to say it won no cooking prize, nor could it be remotely compared to any kind of homestyle meal any of us had ever experienced.

So it was time to dust off the old ploy which had worked on occasion back in California. It was almost tradition for singing groups working on radio to make some kind of offhand mention of food during the course of a broadcast, hoping that someone out there in radioland would get the hint and drop by the station with a cake or a pie or maybe a platefull of fresh-baked cookies—anything but rabbit.

Between songs on the Roswell station the subject of food came up right on cue, and I said something like, "I'd just about give my left arm for a piece of lemon pie like Mom bakes back home." It would prove to be not only my most sincere but best performance of the tour.

No sooner were we off the air than a young lady called and said if I would do "The Swiss Yodel" on the air the following day she would come running with a whole lemon pie. I practiced the song well into the night and, to hurry along delivery as much as possible, opened the next day's show with it. It probably wasn't the best rendition of the song ever done, but I bet it's never been done with more enthusiasm.

When we got off the air, however, there was no young lady, no lemon pie. Spirits collectively fell as we loaded into the car to return to the tourist court. And rose dramatically when, on our arrival, we saw a woman and a young girl standing at our door, each of them holding still-warm lemon pies.

"I'm Mrs. Wilkins from across the street," she said, "and this is my daughter Arlene, who called you at the station. She loved your 'Swiss Yodel.' "

Arlene smiled but didn't say anything. Neither did I. I was standing there with my mouth open, having forgotten about the pies for the moment, looking at the prettiest girl I'd ever seen. Don't ever believe anyone who tries to convince you there's no such thing as love at first sight.

The next day I delivered the empty pie plates to the Wilkins's house, came to the conclusion that she was even prettier than I had first thought, and returned to the group with the welcome news that we had been invited over for fried chicken that evening. Things were looking up.

Mrs. Wilkins's fried chicken dinner was far more successful than the show we eventually put on. We didn't even draw enough people to pay for our lodging. We were finally saved by the local Lions Club, which agreed to let us do a square dance for them. We made enough money to pay our bill at the tourist court and get the repair work done on our car as we traveled into the Texas Panhandle. We reached Lubbock, Texas, then, in a familiar state: so broke we couldn't pay attention.

The less-than-enthusiastic reception there did it. Enough, we decided, was enough. We had made enough money to make it home, so, canceling the remainder of our tour to nowhere, we headed back toward California. Slumber Nichols got himself a job with a radio station in Fort Worth, Tim Spencer went to work for Safeway, sacking groceries, and I joined a group called The Texas Outlaws. When I wasn't working on radio KFWB, I was writing letters to Arlene Wilkins in Roswell, New Mexico.

I kept thinking that it was possible to make a go of being a musician. All you had to do to know that it wasn't impossible was listen to the records they were playing on the radio or go out to see live performances that had seats filled with admission-paying customers.

Allowing him what I considered a proper amount of time to forget some of the hardships of our abortive past efforts, I sought out Tim Spencer. He quickly pointed out to me that he was fast coming to enjoy eating regularly and having a little money in his pocket. It didn't make my mission any easier.

"Tim," I told him, "I want to make one more try at it. I've come too far to stop now. Let's you and me go find Bob Nolan and try it as a trio. I believe we can make it."

Once a musician, always a musician. Tim agreed to have a go at it. So did Bob Nolan. The Pioneer Trio was born and began rehearsing around the clock for its debut on an

early morning show on KFWB with Jack and His Texas Outlaws. Of course, there would be no pay.

But, lo and behold, a man named Bernie Milligan, a columnist for the *Los Angeles Examiner,* put an end to that. Having
heard us on the radio, he touted us in his "Best Bets of the
Day," and suddenly the station agreed to put us on the staff
at thirty-five dollars a week each. We left the Outlaws and
soon were working on a regular basis, earning enough money
to hire staff musicians and add a talented fiddle player named
Hugh Farr.

The Pioneer Trio soon became known as The Sons of the
Pioneers. Whatever it was we were doing was working, and
none of us was about to spoil things with a lot of analyzing.
We picked up a radio sponsor, did an occasional guest spot
on even bigger radio programs, did a little movie background
work, and suddenly weren't having to go hat in hand looking
for playing dates. In fact, we were working almost every night.

One particular show we did comes to mind. There was a
Salvation Army benefit being held in San Bernardino where
Will Rogers, the folksy Oklahoma cowboy who had captured
the nation's heart with his homespun wit, was appearing. Having heard us perform, he had personally asked that we do
the show with him. It was a great thrill to share the stages
with him, and after the show was over we stood around talking
for quite some time.

Finally, he said he had to be going. "Gotta get some rest,"
he said. "Me an' Wiley Post are taking off for Alaska tomorrow."

Little did we know at the time that we had worked with
Will Rogers in his last public appearance. The saddening news
came on August 15, 1935 that he and his pilot Post had died
in a crash near Port Barrow, Alaska. I have since visited that
spot, while on a hunting trip in Alaska.

THE FOLLOWING YEAR the state of Texas was celebrating its
Centennial in Dallas, and the Sons of the Pioneers were invited
by Governor James V. Allred of Texas to entertain the thousands who would come to the State Fair Grounds in Dallas
to join in the festivities.

I wrote Arlene to tell her that we would be coming her

way and offered a suggestion. En route to Dallas, then, I stopped by the Wilkins's house—not for a piece of lemon pie but instead a slice of wedding cake. In the living room of her family's home we were married on June 14, 1936, and went to Dallas to combine our honeymoon with the one-hundredth birthday of Texas.

Ol' Leonard Slye, feeling pretty good about himself, was definitely on a hot streak.

3

IN THE FALL OF 1937 I stopped by a Western hat store in Glendale to see what, if anything, could be done about getting the only cowboy hat I owned cleaned up a bit. It was, frankly, more than a little worse for the wear, but the price of a new one was well out of reach of the Slye family budget. So, to borrow a phrase from Dad, I was making do.

While the clerk looked it over, making me fully aware that he was not in the miracle business but agreeable nonetheless to seeing what he could do, I admired one of the new Stetsons (a model made popular by Tom Mix) he had on display. At that moment a breathless young man, rangy and Western-looking as they come, came running into the store and told the clerk that he needed a new cowboy hat in the worst way.

The sudden prospect of a sale, needless to say, put my cleaning job on the waiting list in a hurry.

"I just heard," the excited customer told the clerk, "that they're gonna hold tests for singing cowboys tomorrow over at Republic. I'm gonna give it a whirl, so I need me a really good-looking hat."

For a brief moment I considered offering him a little friendly advice, but then thought better of it. Even if he knew that having a screen test could end up being one of the biggest disappointments of his life, he would go through with it anyway. So he bought his hat and left, filled with great aspirations. That, folks, is show biz.

A few months earlier I had traveled down the same pie-in-the-sky dream road. The Sons of the Pioneers had steadily grown in popularity and had had a pretty good list of movie credits working. I had even landed a few bit parts here and there in Westerns and comedies—never really doing much acting but, like just about everyone who gets a taste of the movie business, thinking I probably could if the chance ever came along.

I was serious enough about it to adopt a screen name which sounded a little more Western than Leonard Slye. For the life of me I can't tell you why the name Dick Weston was chosen, but you'll have to admit it sounded a little more like a guy who could ride and shoot than the one I was given at birth.

While my parts were generally about as minor as you can get, I did manage to rub elbows with some pretty famous people—Bing Crosby, Dick Foran, Joan Davis, Charlie Starrett, Jo Stafford, Phil Regan—who were among the biggest box office attractions of the thirties. It was pretty heady stuff for a boy from Duck Run, Ohio.

If someone held a gun to my head I wouldn't be able to repeat a line of dialogue or give you the plots of many of the early-day film appearances of Dick Weston, such as they were, but suffice it to say I wasn't riding around on a golden palomino, winning the West, and getting the girl.

For example: In December 1936 Republic Studios gave me a singing part in a movie entitled *The Old Corral,* starring Gene Autry. The plot escapes me, but I do remember having this fight with Gene (guess who was the good guy in that one!). Okay, so Gene wins the fight and then forces me, at gunpoint, to sing him a song. Being a bad guy and all, it was something I was supposed to be completely humiliated by.

Such roles caused no great stir among the members of the Motion Picture Academy, to be sure, but they did serve to reinforce my enthusiasm for the business. Thus when Universal Studios offered me a screen test I was quick to accept. I was sure that Dick Weston, future movie star, was on his way.

A fella named Bob Baker also tested, however, and I finished second in the two-actor race—Trim Carr, the producer, said I photographed too young-looking. I'm afraid I didn't waste a great deal of energy in the next couple of months trying to convince others that I wasn't disappointed about the missed opportunity. I moped around, generally felt sorry for myself, and gradually came to grips with the fact that Leonard Slye by any other name was still Leonard Slye—one of those people destined to go just so far and no farther. I privately lectured myself on the matter and decided that it would be in the best interest of all if I accepted my particular position in life and made the best of it. I vowed to quit looking to greener pastures and courting disappointment.

It wasn't a bad lecture, if I do say so myself. The Pioneers were making headway, I had a pretty lady in my life, and there were still the bit parts in movies from time to time. After our successful engagement in Dallas at the Texas Centennial we had been invited to join Peter Potter's "Hollywood Barn Dance" radio show as regulars. Things were beginning to look pretty satisfactory to me.

Until that young cowboy came barging in to see about buying himself a new hat.

The discussion I had with Arlene that evening is proof positive that time heals the wounds of disappointment. I found myself eagerly telling her of the conversation I had overheard and of my plans to be at Republic Studios the following day.

To her everlasting credit she offered no reminder of the earlier disappointment at Universal. Looking back on it, I guess she saw in me what I had seen a few hours earlier in that young cowboy in the hat shop. Republic was calling and, whether Republic knew it or not, Dick Weston was ready to ride.

It never occurred to me that I would have trouble even getting on the lot. To show you how schooled I was in the ways of Hollywood, I arrived at the Republic gates early the next morning with neither a gate pass nor the foresight not to admit to the guard on duty that I had no appointment. The guard, I have to say, was jealously devoted to his job. No amount of persuading would soften his stance. No, he had never heard of Dick Weston. Never heard of the Sons of the Pioneers. And, nope, he didn't recollect ever seeing me before, even though I had gone through that gate dozens of times.

I got the distinct impression that should I have broken and run for the gate he might well have drygulched me even before I had a chance to strum a note. Fresh out of ideas and unwilling to return home and admit to Arlene that I hadn't even managed the opportunity to fail this time around, I waited. And waited.

For several hours I stood outside that gate, hoping to see a familiar face or, better yet, devise some brilliant plan for getting past the guard. The familiar face, alas, never materialized; finally a plan did. Its brilliance, however, is subject to question.

As a large group of studio employees returned from lunch, strolling past the guard without so much as a wave or show of identification. I fell in with them, head down, trying to look as casual as a trespasser can hope to. I had made it roughly ten yards before my adversary spotted me and called out for me to stop.

Then fate, bless her, took over. Just as I was about to receive my escort off the lot—and, no doubt, out of the motion picture business—I heard a friendly voice. Sol Siegel, the producer, recognized me and came over to say hello. In all the movies I would later make I can't think of a rescue I made that was any more timely than that of Mr. Siegel's.

"Something you want to see us about?" he asked.

Literally with hat in hand, I explained to him about hearing of the screen testing. "I'd like to stay around and try," I said. If the truth were known, I probably was digging the toe of my boot into the ground as I made my pitch. Suffice it to say it probably wasn't the most forceful job application Sol Seigel had ever received.

"Let's go into my office and talk," he said.

Once seated, he lit a cigar and pointed out to me that he had already tested a dozen or so cowboys that day. "I don't know why I didn't think about you," he said. "The job's still open. Where's your guitar? It's a *singing* cowboy I'm looking for, you know."

In another stroke of the genius which seemed set on sabotaging my own chances, I had left the guitar in my car a couple of blocks away. "Well, go get it," Siegel said. I hurried to the door and then turned to speak.

"Don't worry," he said, reading my thoughts, "I'll see that the guard lets you back in."

I ran all the way. I hit the doors of Siegel's office singing. Actually, about all I was able to do was pant and heave to the beat. Siegel smiled and motioned toward a chair. "Sit and get your breath back," he said, "then let's hear you sing."

After a few minutes I sang Bob Nolan's "Tumbling Tumbleweeds," the theme song of the Sons of the Pioneers, then a couple more that we did in just about all our shows, plus some yodeling. Siegel said nothing until I finished, then after what seemed like an eternity to me, rose and smiled. "I think," he said, "you just might be what we're looking for. We'll test you first thing tomorrow."

Then, as something of an afterthought, he said, "You aren't tied up with any other studio, are you?"

The fact of the matter is that I *was* tied up. Along with the rest of the Sons of the Pioneers, I was under contract to Columbia Studios to do background music for their Charles Starrett pictures. I explained it as best I could to Mr. Siegel, and he suggested that there might be some way I could talk them into releasing me.

The people I most needed to talk to, though, were the Pioneers. The problem as I saw it was finding a replacement for myself. Columbia didn't want Leonard Slye or Dick Weston under contract; it simply wanted the background music provided by the Sons of the Pioneers. If they could be assured that my absence wouldn't affect the music, I didn't see any problem.

Which is basically what they told me when I told them of the opportunity. The Pioneers told me not to worry about things, that the chance was too good to pass by. Still, I felt a need to be sure my spot was filled.

It was time to take a drive down the Coast Highway and have a talk with another old Ohio boy I had come to know and respect since moving to the West Coast. Pat Brady was not only a good man to go to for advice, but just might be the solution to the problem.

He played in a string quartet at a restaurant called Sam's Place on Sunset Beach, a spot we often stopped in after a performance. More often than not, we would wind up in a hot jam session after closing time. There were a number of things that impressed me about Brady. First of all, anyone from Ohio couldn't be all bad. Second, he was an accomplished musician, and had been in show business of one form or another since he was just a toddler following his mother and father, traveling tent show performers, from town to town. And third, I guess if I had ever run across anyone more shy than myself at the time, it was Pat Brady.

I came straight to the point with him after completing the fifty-mile drive. I outlined the situation and then said, "Pat, I can't guarantee that things will work out between you and the Pioneers, but if you would give it a try it would be a big favor to me. With you as my replacement, I would be free to test for the Republic contract."

He agreed. The Pioneers agreed. Columbia agreed. And on October 13, 1937, I signed a contract with Republic Studios.

There are varying theories as to why Republic would sign me or, for that matter, any other singing cowboy, to a contract when it did. It already had Gene Autry, who in 1937 was solidly the number-one box office draw among Western stars. Already a veteran of twenty-four movies, he was as familiar a name as Hollywood had to offer. To introduce a new singing cowboy, some said, would put the studio in competition with itself.

But others suggest that Autry's success had motivated Republic to increase its production of Westerns and therefore command an even larger income. Then there was the theory that Gene was becoming dissatisfied with some of Republic's policies, and was threatening to strike for higher wages if the studio did not agree to some of his demands.

To this day I'm not sure what the basic motivation in hiring me was. I do know, however, that the hardest part of my new job in the early days was sitting around waiting for something to happen. Not only did I spend the first several months just reporting to the studio to stand around and do nothing, I found out that just about everything about me was wrong. Someone, for instance, decided that my shoulders weren't broad enough, so I was placed on a routine which called for a hundred handstands a day. The fitting department put extra padding into my shirts. They even talked about some kind of drops for my eyes to make me squint less.

I did finally sing a solo in a film entitled *The Three Mesquiteers,* the first of a lengthy series of Three Mesquiteers Westerns which starred Ray Corrigan, Robert Livingston, and Max Terhune. It sure beat doing a hundred handstands a day, but the fan mail didn't exactly start flooding in. I was a long way from being King of the Cowboys.

Then Gene Autry declined to show up on the first day of shooting a new picture.

In his own biography, *Back in the Saddle Again,* Gene points to a number of reasons for his decision. His contract included a clause which entitled Republic Studios to half the money he received from things like endorsements, radio, or public appearances. And then, he was quite upset over the fact that the studio had begun to confront film distributors with a block buying proposition—to get one of Gene's pictures they had to agree to take a number of other Republic films. For a number of the smaller distributors this jumped the price of the package to an amount their relatively slim budgets could not stand. Some were no longer able to purchase the Autry movies that their customers, the movie houses, wanted.

It was, according to Gene, the block buying scheme which was the final straw. He reportedly confronted Republic owner Herb Yates with his list of grievances—he wanted the block buying practice stopped, the clause allowing the studio to pocket half his nonmovie earnings removed, and, while he was at it, a fairer share of the profits from his increasingly successful films.

But Herbert J. Yates was not a man who had gotten where

he was by bowing to the wishes of those he had under contract. At one time he owned Consolidated Film Labs, a processing plant which was developing the majority of films shot by Hollywood studios. It was pretty common practice in those days for Yates and Consolidated Film Labs to develop film for smaller studios—companies like Monogram, Mascot, Liberty, Majestic, Imperial, and Chesterfield, whose main fare was low-budget serials and adventure movies—on promise of payment later.

Then one day in 1935 came the announcement of a merger—the aforementioned studios would form a new corporation to be known as Republic Pictures, Inc. Merger it wasn't. Consolidated Film Labs had simply made an immediate demand for all money owed it, and Yates was suddenly in the motion-picture business in a big way. He inherited Mascot's North Hollywood studio and the contracts of a couple of pretty valuable properties—Ann Rutherford and Gene Autry. From Monogram he got the contract of a young Western star named John Wayne.

There are those who credit Herb Yates with the foresight to add a new twist to the standard Western movies being produced; the idea of a singing cowboy, I'm told, was that of Mr. Yates. And while he and I would have our own misunderstandings in the years to come, be aware that he was a man who well knew how to turn all the keys to success in the movie business.

Word got around pretty quickly that Yates was in absolutely no frame of mind to lose out in a power struggle with Gene Autry or any other person whose check he signed. Not wishing to get involved, and unaware that the incident would have any effect on my career—such as it was—I just kept my mouth shut and did my one hundred handstands a day.

When I was given another bit part in a Gene Autry movie entitled *The Old Barn Dance,* I had no way of knowing it would be his last for Republic for over six months. The meetings in Yates's office had evidently resulted in both parties refusing to budge. When Gene failed to show up on the first scheduled day of shooting for a movie to be called *Washington Cowboy,* he was suspended. The studio even took out an injunction to prevent his appearing on stage until his contract with Republic had been fulfilled.

Like I said, Herb Yates drove a pretty hard bargain.

I don't mind telling you I was more than a little nervous when I was summoned to his office. And I couldn't tell you what I said when he informed me that I was going to play the lead in the movie Gene had failed to show up for. The truth of it was that I was speechless.

Washington Cowboy was something of a Western's answer to *Mr. Smith Goes to Washington*. The script had a cowboy take the Dust Bowl story to the men in Congress, appealing for help for the ranchers whose cattle were dying and farmers whose crops were burning up in the fields. And there was also a nest of local politicians who had been bought body and soul by the evil and oppressive water company to be dealt with. So, quite naturally, the powers-that-be decided to change the name of the picture to *Under Western Stars*. In my years in the movie business I feel like I have learned a few things here and there. But, for the life of me, I have never managed to come to an understanding of the manner in which film titles are decided upon.

At that particular time, though, I wasn't in the least concerned over what title would eventually be flashed across the screen. The simple fact that I was going to actually start working for my seventy-five dollars per week made everything else quite secondary.

But before the shooting finally got underway, there were still a few details to be ironed out. My physical appearance was evidently finally satisfactory (they even gave up on the idea of the drops for my eyes), but it was decided that my name was still wrong. Dick Weston, it was decreed, wasn't all that much of an improvement over Leonard Slye. So the Republic brain trust went into a huddle.

Yates gathered several of the studio's top men—Bill Saal, and Moe and Sol Siegel—into his office and began the search for the proper name for Republic's new singing cowboy. Sol Siegel, I was later told, pointed to the fact that the late Will Rogers remained one of the most familiar and best-loved figures in America. "Rogers is a good, solid name," Siegel said. "To the public it represents honesty and integrity and trust. I say let's go with it. The first name has to be something short, easy to remember, but something with some meaning."

"What about something that might offer a little bit of an alliterative ring to it?" Yates suggested.

"*Roy* means 'king,' " Siegel suggested. "How does the name Roy Rogers strike you?"

"I like it," Yates said, rising from the chair behind his desk. That was it. Roy Rogers it was. If anyone had ever bothered to ask, I would probably have said I liked it too.

If nothing else, that particular brainstorming session brought an end to the name game I had already grown tired of playing. Of course, the new name took a little getting used to. But later, in 1942, I went down to the court house and went through the process required by law to have my name legally changed to Roy Rogers.

Once the problem of a name was settled, it was the publicity department's turn. I posed for more pictures than I'd ever posed for in my life, and was repeatedly informed that I had to have what was called a proper "image." Roy Rogers, it was decided, was a true-blue son of the West, born in Cody, Wyoming, and raised on a sprawling cattle ranch. He even was supposed to have labored as a ranchhand in New Mexico for a while before finally making his way to the bright lights of Hollywood. Pictures and press releases soon began going out, introducing the studio's "newest Western star" even before he had gotten far enough down the road to stardom to learn his lines for the movie in which he would debut.

It didn't take long for some of the publicity to backfire. There came a letter to the studio from a complaining group in Cody which seemed far more concerned with historical accuracy than Hollywood hype. Their research, they claimed, revealed absolutely no evidence of anyone named Roy Rogers having ever been born in the whole state of Wyoming, much less Cody.

To the best of my knowledge, the calling of the publicity department's hand did little if anything to slow the flow of advance stories. They had a product to sell, and if it meant a slight alteration of fact and the nation's history now and then, so be it. After all, that, in a nut shell, was what B-Westerns were all about in the first place, so why should the folks in the publicity department tamper with success?

During the filming of *Under Western Stars* I did everything you can think of that an actor is not supposed to do. I forgot my lines, I repeatedly made a mess of my make-up jobs, and I seemed to have a special knack for doing the wrong thing at the wrong time. If the script called for me to draw my gun and say, "Reach!" more often than not I said "Reach!" and *then* drew my gun.

I marveled at the patience of not only Joe Kane, the director, but of the film crew and experienced performers like Carol Hughes and Smiley Burnette, my leading lady and sidekick in the movie. No doubt there were times when they all collectively wished I had stayed on that Wyoming ranch the publicity department had invented for me.

But we got it done and, to the surprise of even the ever-optimistic Herb Yates, the movie was a roaring success. In addition to doing very well at the box office, *Under Western Stars* would eventually be voted the Best Western of the Year.

And I kept learning my lessons about show business. Making a movie is only part of the work for an actor. The next step is to pack your bags and follow it all over the country, making public appearances and promoting it. I would soon learn that my previous musical travels were little more than short distance warm-ups for the travel involved in promoting a movie.

Under Western Stars, a movie made in Hollywood, starring a so-called Wyoming cowboy who goes to Washington, premiered in April of 1938 at the Capitol Theater in—where else?—Dallas, Texas. Figure that bit of logic out.

I'll have to admit, though, that if the people of Dallas did see illogic to our being there, they hid their feelings very well. It was red carpet every step of the way. Smiley and I were presented the keys to the city by the mayor. There were elaborate receptions for us everywhere we went and, best of all, a standing-room-only crowd at the theater.

The studio had hired the Sons of the Pioneers, Pat Brady and all, to make the trip with us since the group had been a great success at the Texas Centennial, and we put on a lengthy stage show before the initial showing of the movie.

The reporters turned out in force for interviews and pictures. And it was in the *Dallas Morning News* that I got my first review. If I wasn't already hooked on the movie business, the reviewer did the trick.

"The movie," the reviewer wrote, "introduces young Mr. Rogers as a new cowboy hero, real out-west and not drugstore variety. This lad isn't the pretty-boy type, but a clean-cut youngster who looks as if he had grown up on the prairies, not backstage with a mail order cowboy suit. An engaging smile, a good voice and an easy manner ought to put him out in front before very long."

Pretty heady stuff, you'll have to agree, for a farm boy from Duck Run, Ohio.

THE LINES OF PEOPLE waiting in front of theaters across the country to see Under Western Stars, *which would earn the distinction of being the first B-Western ever shown at the Criterion Theater on Broadway, not only promised overwhelming financial reward for Republic, but were proof positive that young Roy Rogers was an instant success. On the screen he had been heroic; on the stages of the promotional tour, he had been charming. The moviegoing nation had adopted a new hero.*

The two biggest Roy Rogers fans, Andy and Mattie Slye, followed their son's picture from town to town, feeling a new flow of parental pride every time the words "starring Roy Rogers" appeared on the screen. Their son, fearing they would wreck the family budget buying gasoline and movie tickets, finally arranged to have a print of the film sent to them.

Upon his triumphant return to the studio, he was escorted to the mail room, where stacks of fan mail awaited him. With one feature role Roy Rogers had, in the vernacular of show business, become a star.

With Arlene's help he began the endless task of answering the mail, which seemed to arrive in greater volume each day. Daily she went to the post office with boxes of cards and autographed pictures of her husband to be sent not only to adoring youngsters throughout the country but to people of all ages.

"That," says Roy, "gives you some kind of an indication what kind of a businessman I was. On the salary I was making,

I couldn't even pay for the postage. Finally, I went to Herb Yates and told him about the problem, hoping that maybe the studio would agree to help me handle some of it. He wasted little time telling me that I was foolish to worry about answering fan mail; that nobody else in the business did it because it took too much time and money.

"I couldn't buy that. It seemed to me that if someone is thoughtful enough to sit down and write you a letter, you had an obligation to answer them. Thus, it was obvious to me pretty quickly that I would have to solve the problem myself. Fortunately, the success of the movie had put me in demand."

Taking advantage of the situation, Roy arranged a series of one-night appearances, using the money he earned to help defray his mailing expenses. For the first two years at Republic, in fact, the cost of handling his fan mail exceeded the salary the studio was paying him.

He traveled a lot of miles to buy stamps, pay for pictures, and pay the salaries of four ladies hired to help see that requests were answered.

"In those days," he remembers, *"a theater would pay one hundred fifty dollars for a night's performance. So as soon as I finished a picture, a couple of musicians and I would climb in the car and hit the road. One trip we made comes to mind and serves as a pretty good example of what we did. Over a three-month period we went through Georgia, Virginia, West Virginia, North and South Carolina, Mississippi, Louisiana, Alabama and Tennessee. We'd drive all night and then sometimes do as many as four shows, grab a bite to eat, and climb back in the car.*

"The more I traveled, the more disgusted I became with the studio. I had been made aware that there were other studios which were agreeing to help with the fan mail, realizing that those people who were writing were also buying tickets to the movies.

"Once, when I got back off the road dead tired, I got so disgusted with the whole thing that I hired a five ton dump truck, filled it with mail and drove over to the studio. I backed it up to the front of Herb Yates's office and dumped it on the lawn.

"He came running out, waving his hands and yelling, asking

what I thought I was doing. I just smiled and told him it was some of the fan mail that he wouldn't help me to answer, and that I was just about killing myself trying to do it on my own."

Yates, flabbergasted, was momentarily speechless. Then as Roy climbed back into the cab of the truck the studio owner said, "You're not going to just leave all this here, are you?"

"Yes sir," Roy said politely, driving away.

The grandstand play had all the elements of first-class theatrics but, in truth, did little good. As mail addressed to Roy Rogers increased to twenty thousand letters a week, Herb Yates stood his ground. Except for the fact that he agreed to increase Roy's salary by twenty-five dollars a week. Two years after signing his contract with Republic, he was making one hundred fifty dollars a week—and still doing one-nighters like they were going out of style.

4

THE THUNDERING SUCCESS of Under Western Stars *left little question that the familiar Republic eagle was going to fly quite nicely, even if Gene Autry never came to terms. He later did, of course, but the studio wasted little time getting four more Roy Rogers pictures into the movie houses in 1938.*

Herb Yates, knowing a good thing when he saw it, instructed his directors to provide his newest singing cowboy with a strong cast of supporting actors and actresses, to see that the scripts were meaningful and that the songs were selected to best benefit the engaging style of his new star. So successful had been the previously unused twist of having a star play himself in his pictures (even the legendary Tom Mix never played a part which called for his real name to be used in the plot) that the studio made plans to keep it that way.

Roy's second starring role came in Billy the Kid Returns,

an action-filled story which begins with the death of the legend-
ary outlaw at the hands of Pat Garret and then switches to
Roy Rogers who, by decree of the scriptwriters, had the misfor-
tune of being the spitting image of the Kid. You can imagine
the problems that causes an otherwise easygoing, clean-cut sing-
ing cowboy.

To add a touch of romance, Lynn Roberts was cast in the
female lead, and again Gene Autry's old sidekick, Smiley Bur-
nette, provided the comedy. The Rogers–Roberts combination
was ideal, the Republic brain trust agreed, but the name of
Roy's leading lady gave Yates problems. The story goes that
Yates, an unabashed fan of the Broadway success of Rogers
and Hart musicals, decreed that Lynn Roberts would henceforth
be known as Mary Hart and that his own Western version of
Rogers and Hart would be billed as the "Sweethearts of the
West."

That lasted for six pictures. Then B-Westerns began to wear
on Miss Hart, who decided to reclaim her old name and seek
other avenues of artistic expression.

By 1939 Burnette was back playing fall guy to Gene Autry,
and a search was on for a new sidekick for Rogers. The role,
briefly filled by Raymond Hatton, eventually fell to George
"Gabby" Hayes, who had finally managed to get out of a con-
tract which called for him to play the role of Windy Halliday,
an old codger teamed with Bill Boyd in the highly popular
Hopalong Cassidy series. Deep personal conflicts had devel-
oped between Hayes and Boyd, however, and once released
Hayes signed with Republic. He joined Smiley Burnette in a
couple of Autry movies before the studio teamed him with
Roy.

It would be the beginning of a fruitful professional relation-
ship and, perhaps even more important, a longstanding friend-
ship. They would remain close friends long after their movie
partnership ended. Until his death at age eighty-four, Hayes
was a frequent house guest of Roy and Dale.

GABBY WAS LIKE A FATHER—a buddy and a brother to me.
People never realized what an exceptional actor he was. He
was born in Wellsville, New York, and was working vaudeville

when he was just a kid. He and his wife, a dancer, married when they were sixteen or seventeen years old, and worked on the stage together for years before he ever came out to Hollywood.

The Gabby Hayes people saw on the screen and the real man weren't anything alike. I'll never forget the first time I saw him. He came driving onto the lot in this big Lincoln convertible, dressed to the teeth. In fact, he was easily one of the best dressed men in Hollywood. But he would go into his dressing room, take out his teeth, and put on his old western clothes and hat. He would come out walking stooped over and suddenly he was Gabby Hayes.

In his early film days, when he was working with people like John Wayne in his early Westerns, playing the heavy a lot, he was known simply as George Hayes and didn't have a trace of a chin whisker. But in his later years he really became quite proud of that bushy beard of his.

I remember once going on a fishing trip between pictures. I came back to find I had an urgent message to call Gabby as soon as possible. I called right away, and the first thing he said was, "Roy, there was almost a disaster while you were gone. For some dang crazy reason I got it into my mind to shave my beard off, and after I'd done it I almost died. I don't remember myself looking so ugly. But don't worry; things are getting better. It's growing out real fast. So don't get concerned if you don't see me for a while. I'm not even gonna stick my head out the door until the dang thing's grown back and I look myself again."

He was one of those actors who saw the need for a particular identity, and settled on the Gabby Hayes look. It made him a rich man before he finally called it a career.

There was only one critic to whom he paid any attention at all. As soon as one of our pictures would come out he would take his wife to see it. The next day, depending on her judgment, he would come around all excited or down in the dumps. "Maw really liked that one," he would say, or "Maw didn't really care much for that one."

He was always telling us about his angina problem but, for some reason, it never seemed to crop up until he had trouble with a scene or missed a cue or said his lines wrong. When that would happen—which was very seldom—he would grab his chest and say he had to rest for a few minutes. I'd always help him to a chair and say, "Take it easy for a few minutes, Pappy, and you'll be okay." The next thing you knew he was smiling and jumping around and ready to go.

When his wife died, Gabby died a little too. He just never had that old enthusiasm again. Once when I hadn't seen him for quite some time, I got word that he was pretty sick, so I drove over to his house. He was lying in bed—it was evident that he hadn't been eating—and he talked about how badly his angina was bothering him. At that point I honestly didn't know if he was really all that sick or just mourning Maw's death. So I got on him pretty good and told him to get up and get dressed because I wanted him to go out to the gun club and shoot a few skeet. He brightened up, smiled, and said, "Roy, I was beginning to think you never were gonna get here."

He became a very lonely man in the years after his wife died, though. I'll never forget one evening when he came over to have dinner with us. Sitting there at our table, looking around at our family, he just broke down and cried.

It DIDN'T take me too many personal appearances, promoting the movies we were making, to learn one of the basic requirements a movie cowboy was duty-bound to fulfill before he would be completely accepted. William S. Hart, the pioneer Western star, had set the precedent when his pinto Fritz became almost as popular with audiences as he was. Hopalong had Topper, Tom Mix had Tony, Gene Autry had Champion, Ken Maynard would share billing with Tarzan, The Wonder Horse.

And I was renting Trigger at that time.

It was customary for most of the studios to lease horses for whatever picture they were shooting, and there were a number of stables in southern California turning a nice profit in the business. They had a large herd of stock horses which could be used for pulling wagons or standing around in corrals or serving as part of a wild horse herd. They had gentle horses for novice riders, more spirited ones for the actors able to handle them, and trained ones whose specialties went hand in glove with the tumbles and daredevil work of the stuntmen. The ones with the best breeding and classiest markings were leased for the benefit of the star of the picture. They were called cast horses.

They went back to the rental stable after the filming was completed, so there I was making tours with no horse trailer in tow. At virtually every stop, people would ask, "Where's your horse, cowboy?" We rented my palomino from Hudkins, one of the stables Republic did considerable business with. So I drove out there one day and, after quite a bit of horse trading, bought him for twenty-five hundred dollars.

It was the beginning of a cowboy and horse partnership which lasted until the horse's death in 1965, at the age of thirty-three. His palomino registered name was Golden Cloud, but the Golden Cloud name went the way of Leonard Slye. I had already decided to name him Trigger.

I wanted Trigger to be able to run through a few simple tricks for a rodeo appearance in Baltimore scheduled just over a month away. So I got in touch with Glenn Randall, a former rodeo performer who had the reputation of being an expert horse trainer. Unlike so many trainers who reward horses with cubes of sugar after they have properly followed their cue, Glenn explained to me that a pat, a kind word, and perhaps an occasional carrot would get the trick done just as well. "And," he added, "once you've got the horse trained you don't have a beggar on your hands." He would later tell me he was amazed at the quickness with which Trigger learned.

I was learning a few things too. After I had more or less established myself as a Western actor, Herb Yates came to me with a script he wanted me to study. Republic was planning to shoot a movie entitled *Front Page,* and Yates wanted me to play the part of a cocky newspaper reporter. It just didn't make sense to me to suddenly switch my image just after I had begun to establish myself in Westerns. So we got into a pretty heated argument which resulted in my telling him in no uncertain terms that I wasn't going to do the part.

"In that case," he said, "maybe we'll just have to put some other cowboy on Trigger and let him do your next movie."

Like I said, Herb Yates always had an angle.

"You may get someone to do the next picture," I told him, "but he won't be riding Trigger. I bought him."

Once aware that the horse belonged to me, Mr. Yates signed Lloyd Nolan for the part in *Front Page,* and I went on about my business of being a singing cowboy.

Herb Yates never really gave up the idea of my working in other pictures, though, and we would go through the same old argument every time. I did do one in 1940 that was a far cry from being a B-Western, playing a hot-headed scalawag in a movie entitled *Dark Command,* directed by Raoul Walsh. Gabby, who also had a strong role in the movie, had a part in persuading me to do the picture. We were in pretty good company, with a cast that included John Wayne, Walter Pidgeon, Claire Trevor, and Marjorie Main.

I felt far more comfortable in the saddle, however, and was back to films like *Red River Valley* and *Carson City Kid* long before *Dark Command* premiered to good reviews and packed houses.

Trigger liked me back in Westerns, too, since he was being billed as the "Smartest Horse in the Movies" and was even being written into many of the scripts. In years to come, in fact, he would receive as many as two hundred pieces of fan mail a week, and would be insured for one hundred thousand dollars.

After my first couple of years in the movie business, Arlene and I were still counting our pennies, living in a little frame house, and wondering where the money we had heard movie stars were supposed to be making was. I had tried to supplement my income by opening a Western apparel store called The Hitching Post in Studio City, but about all that venture had proven was that as a businessman I made a pretty fair cowboy.

It was the end of 1939. I had made thirteen pictures, and was constantly worried about making it to the next paycheck. If, when I first met a man named Art Rush, I had known what he would be able to do for me in the years to come, I would probably have given him a big hug rather than a skeptical handshake.

MY LUCK with agents had been holding—all bad—when I received a call at the studio from a man who identified himself as a specialist in talent management. He suggested it might be beneficial to us both if we could meet at lunch. At the time I had already had a couple of informal discussions with a representative from the William Morris Agency, and had pretty well decided to sign a contract with them whenever we could work out the details. But Art Rush persisted, so I suggested we meet at Eaton's, a restaurant just across the street from Republic.

I didn't see that I had anything to lose, since he promised to pick up the tab.

Art Rush was one of those people who arrived on the West Coast with his sleeves rolled up and wasted no time making a mark for himself. By age twenty-five, he was already the youngest executive in the RCA Victor organization, producing records for a virtual Who's Who in the music industry— Benny Goodman, Tommy Dorsey, Arthur Rubinstein, Nelson Eddy, Jeanette MacDonald. You get the idea; there were no O-Bar-O Cowboy castoffs in his stable.

In 1937 he founded and became managing director of Columbia Management of California. A subsidiary of the Columbia Broadcasting System, Columbia Management combined eight New York talent agencies and the CBS Artists Bureau into one of the world's largest talent agencies providing musical stars for motion pictures, radio, recordings, and concerts. At one point over two hundred of the nation's biggest names in music fell under Rush's direction.

And here he was trying to convince me he was interested in becoming my manager.

Art would later explain to me that, having tired of the corporate rat race, he had decided to go into business for himself, maintaining a small group of performers to represent. At the time he called me he was managing Nelson Eddy, a star at MGM and of the famous Chase and Sanborn radio show. Also, he had the Sportsman Quartet on the Jack Benny radio program. He explained to me that he needed a Western singer-actor to make the list complete. It occurred to me that he needed me about like he needed a hole in the head. I mean, there's a pretty wide stretch of ground between a Nelson Eddy and a one hundred fifty-dollar-a-week singing cowboy.

"I'm familiar with your work," he said, "and I like it. My intention is to not have any clients whose careers would be in conflict. I have no one remotely in your kind of work, and I understand you are looking for a manager . . ."

I explained to him that I had already spoken with the William Morris Agency and felt a moral obligation to go with them. To my surprise and relief, he pressed the issue no farther. Instead, we spent the rest of lunch just talking. Agent or no agent, he was one of the most likable people I had come in contact with in the business.

As we got ready to leave I reached in my pocket for a tip and asked, "Where are you from?"

"Ohio," he said. "I'm just a small-town boy. Even had a pony and horse myself when I was a kid. I can ride."

That did it. So much for William Morris and moral obligations. "Mr. Rush," I said, "we've got ourselves a deal."

To this day that handshake over a table at Eaton's is the closest thing to a contract Art Rush and I have ever had. It's been that way for thirty-eight years. In that time he not only has been the only manager I've ever had, but my best friend as well. Still, I've never let him forget that he wasn't altogether truthful on that day we shook hands for the first time.

To his credit, he did grow up in Ohio, but I would later find out he was actually born in Pennsylvania.

"THE FIRST THING I HAD TO DO," Art Rush remembers, "was to find some way to begin making Roy some money. I couldn't believe it when I found out what the studio was paying him. Here was a young man who had already established himself as a star, yet was having a pretty hard time making ends meet.

"Since he had already signed a seven-year contract with Republic, there was nothing to do but see if we couldn't get him some public appearances other than the ones which were being set up through the studio. I went to Republic and they agreed.

"Then I got Roy a couple of half-hour transcription radio shows—a drama called 'Manhattan Cowboy'—to be syndicated

to radio stations across the country (the last we heard, they had been repeated ninety-three times on KFI in Los Angeles alone). Next I went to James Osborne, an investment counselor who handled Nelson Eddy's affairs, and asked him to see what he could do about salvaging Roy's Hitching Post Western apparel store. James, I think, found it a little strange to be working on behalf of a client who appeared to have absolutely no need for an investment counselor. 'Just give it a little time,' I told him."

The extra hundred dollars Roy earned from his efforts as the "Manhattan Cowboy" gave him reason to believe Rush was, indeed, the guiding spirit his career needed. When he launched into a series of personal appearances at rodeos across the country (Madison Square Garden being the first major one), earning fees he had never considered possible, he was certain of it.

In short order, the work that he was doing away from Republic Studio was earning him far more than his acting job. Still, he knew, his appearances in the movies were opening the doors on which Art Rush was so successfully knocking.

For Rush, it was exciting just to watch the eagerness and enthusiasm his new client brought to his work. His interest in Roy Rogers went far beyond the normal Hollywood client-agent relationship. "He was, and still is, the most genuine, down-to-earth person I've ever had the pleasure of knowing. Being associated with Roy and his family over the years has been the richest experience I could ever hope for."

The steady schedule of personal appearances was adding to an income now being watched over by James Osborne, a man who would eventually become Roy's personal business manager. Rush went to his client with good news.

"Roy," he said, "I think you're now in a position where you and Arlene can move out of that little frame house."

"How much do you think I can afford to spend?" Roy asked.

"Jim says you can afford something in the ten thousand dollar range."

Those were the words Roy had been wanting to hear for quite some time. He immediately began a search for the place he had in mind and finally located it in the San Fernando

Valley. There was a small chicken ranch, complete with 3,500 chickens and a comfortable white bungalow on the property. He told a puzzled Jim Osborne to close the deal as quickly as possible.

Once all the papers were signed, Roy picked up Andy and Mattie Slye and drove them out to see it. As they stood on the porch, Roy handed his father the key to the front door. "Welcome home, Dad," he said. "You're gonna be getting all the sunshine you want now, tending to all those chickens."

Inside Mattie found a large bolt of material. "I figured you would want to make your own curtains," her son said.

"He had never mentioned anything about it as far as I know," remembers Art Rush, "but buying that home for his folks was something he had planned for a long time. He didn't do it with a lot of fanfare, but he did it with class. The place hadn't taken all the ten thousand dollars I had told him he could afford, so he used the balance to fill a dozen sugar bowls with cash and put them in his mother's pantry where she would find them later.

"I knew right then that this man Roy Rogers was going to be a pleasure to do business with. He had purchased the ranch for his Mom and Dad before he bought a home for Arlene and himself."

ART MADE SURE no grass grew under my feet. If I wasn't working on a picture or on the road promoting one or doing my radio show, he had me doing personal appearances somewhere.

In 1941, one of those trips took me several places. In Louisville, Kentucky, I was entertaining at an orphanage. A beautiful little girl about three years old hung onto my neck all the way through the place. When I got ready to leave, she was still clinging to me, and as the nurse took her away she was crying, "Take me with you, take me with you!"

I never got over that. Arlene and I had been wanting very much to begin a family, but things didn't seem to be working out. We had, in fact, already begun to talk some about adoption. So on my way home from Louisville, I stopped at the Republic Pictures Exchange in Dallas, Texas, and I asked Bob O'Donnell and Bill Underwood if they knew where I could adopt a child.

They said, "You came to the right place." They were on the Board of Directors of Hope Cottage, a home for orphaned and abandoned children. We arranged to meet Mrs. Carson that afternoon.

There were forty-two babies at the Cottage at that time. I started through and got to about the fifth bed, where a pair of little eyes looked right at me. I never had to look any further. I knew God had worked in a wondrous way and had given us our first child—a beautiful little girl with curly blonde hair and the prettiest brown eyes you ever saw. I told Mrs. Carson on the spot that I wanted the baby.

As soon as I returned to the hotel from Hope Cottage I called home. Arlene was just as excited as I was, asking if I was going to be able to bring her home with me right away. "No," I said, "we have to wait until she's four months old. And the people here have to check some things out; make sure we're going to provide her a good home."

We talked for some time, laying plans, laughing, and discussing what it was going to be like to have a child around the house. I was preparing to hang up when Arlene asked a question that had skipped her mind in the excitement: "Roy, what's her name?"

"Cheryl Darlene," I said. "Pretty, isn't it?"

"It most certainly is," she replied.

The people at Hope Cottage were cooperative, kind—and more thorough than bank examiners. They sent a representative to California to meet Arlene and look at our home—she stayed two weeks with us. We answered question after question, hoping to assure the representative that we were the right parents for little Cheryl, that we weren't the "motion picture type" people so many expect to find in Hollywood.

When Cheryl was four months old, Arlene and I drove to Dallas to pick her up. Anxious to play the proud father role, I suggested a stop in Lubbock, Texas, on the way home to say hello to Tim Spencer's wife Velma, who was there visiting her parents.

Velma, of course, was delighted about the adoption. Others, however, weren't. Republic Studio's publicity department threw up its hands and immediately predicted the death of Roy Rogers at the box office as soon as a couple of columnists got wind of the adoption. Until the news appeared that Cheryl had joined our family, no publicity had even mentioned the fact that I was married. For reasons I'll never be able to explain, it was the unwritten Code of Hollywood that stars—male and female alike—should be presented as unmarried and eligible, that otherwise nobody would buy tickets to see their movies. It was and is one of the business's most phony notions.

The way I saw it, we had just gained another Roy Rogers fan.

WITH THE RELEASE of Red River Valley, *a film which saw Roy Rogers reunited with the Sons of the Pioneers, he had completed his twenty-sixth starring role. And while attendance at the nation's movie houses remained good, there was a real-life action drama unfolding which was the primary concern of Americans everywhere.*

The bombing of Pearl Harbor on a December Sunday in 1941 turned everyone's world upside down.

Like so many other members of the entertainment industry, Roy Rogers immediately began making appearances at rallies designed to help sell war bonds and build national morale. He worked tirelessly in behalf of the Red Cross and the Community War Fund Drives. During one tour of Texas for the Eighth Service Command, Roy and Trigger made one hundred thirty-six appearances in the course of a twenty-day period. The United States Department of the Treasury issued him a citation for his efforts, which had resulted in the sale of a million dollars' worth of War Bonds.

Despite his 1-A classification, he would never enter active service. Just as Art Rush was closing out his affairs and canceling further bookings prior to his client's anticipated induction, word came that the age limit of servicemen had been lowered. Thus Roy remained stateside, appearing at benefits, urging his fans to help with scrap metal drives and the multitude of other civilian responsibilities the war had created.

Still there was time for him to continue his motion picture work. And to finally purchase a new home for himself and Arlene—a quiet six-acre spot in the San Fernando Valley which, at one time or another, had been owned by such entertainment world luminaries as W. C. Fields and Martha Raye.

When he signed the papers in 1942, the name he used for legal purposes was no longer Leonard Slye. It was in that year that he had his name legally changed to Roy Rogers. From that day on, only Mattie Slye would refer to him as Leonard. Mothers are that way about things.

ONE OF THE THINGS I had really missed since coming to California was having some good hunting dogs around. As far back as I can remember, there had always been plenty of dogs around, ready to spend the night chasing foxes or treeing raccoons at the drop of a whistle. So one of the first things I did when we moved was get in touch with some people I knew to be avid hunters and start rounding up some dogs. It wasn't hard. Counting the sizable number of strays that wandered up looking for a handout and wound up staying, the number grew to almost twenty before I knew it.

They would be far less trouble than the young man who was to become my number-one hunting partner.

Aside from the people directly associated with the motion picture business, I doubt that you could find many people who can tell you who Carl Switzer was. On the other hand, ask if they are familiar with Alfalfa, the gangly, freckle-faced kid in the "Our Gang" and "Little Rascals" comedies, and it would probably be hard to find anyone who *didn't* know who he was.

Few people, in fact, even called him Carl. To everyone he was Alphie. When I met him he was sixteen or seventeen, his days as a child star behind him. But, believe me when I tell you he was still a rascal. Lovable, friendly, a great guy to be around—when you weren't seriously considering wringing his neck.

For instance: There was the time he came to me all excited about a bear hunt he had organized. A sizable group of hunters had, he explained, agreed to pay him a hundred dollars apiece if he would lead their expedition and furnish the dogs. "Roy," he said, "I can make a killing on this deal if you'll loan me your dogs."

Not only did I agree to loan him the dogs; I suggested he take my Jeep. Somewhere along the way Alphie met a girl, fell madly in love (something he did with great regularity), and found it necessary to sell not only my Jeep but my best lead dog to finance his romance. It was a while before Alphie came around after that.

But, as always, he eventually did, apologizing profusely, and I wound up telling him it was okay. Like I said, he was one of my best hunting buddies.

Like so many highly successful child actors who were supposed to come into big money when they turned twenty-one, Alphie found out when the time finally came that the money was already gone. He had quite a few small parts in movies during his adult years, and even did a couple of episodes of the television show Dale and I later did. But he was never happy for any length of time. Except when we were out hunting. That, to him, was the greatest thing in the world.

We were friends and hunting companions for fifteen years before he died in 1959, shot to death in an argument over thirty dollars he thought some guy owed him for taking care of his dogs. I guess you could say he was like a knot-headed kid you love in spite of his knot-headedness. There was just no way to not like him, no way to stay mad at him.

I was out of town when he died. To this day I can't help but wonder if maybe I'd been around to talk to him before he barged into that man's house and got himself killed for a lousy thirty dollars, things might have turned out differently. Every now and then, when I get the hunting urge, I miss ol' Alphie. Thirty dollars. Such a waste.

THERE MUST HAVE BEEN something about the San Fernando Valley air that agreed with Arlene. Just before Trigger and I were to leave for New York to take part in a victory parade connected with the war effort, I was telling her that the city of New York had waived a longstanding no-horse regulation so I could ride Trigger right between the cars of the governor and mayor.

In retrospect, it was pretty mild news compared to hers. She was, at long last, pregnant. On April 18, 1943, the Rogers family grew to include a sister for Cheryl. With the arrival of Linda Lou, I was outnumbered by females three-to-one.

Considering they were three of the best-looking women in Hollywood, however, I had absolutely no complaints.

5

WITH THE RELEASE of a movie bearing the same title in 1943, Roy Rogers officially became the movie world's "King of the Cowboys." In that busy year he would easily become Hollywood's number-one Western star at the nation's box offices, a position he would keep a firm grip on for the next dozen years. His career was moving fast and in fast company. Along with such motion picture celebrities as James Cagney, Loretta Young, Edgar Bergen, famed British stage actor Sir Cedric Hardwicke, and band leader Fred Waring, he was invited to the White House for a March of Dimes ball held in honor of President Franklin Roosevelt's sixty-first birthday.

While most of those in attendance were carefully abiding by the formal protocol of such an occasion, Roy and First Lady Eleanor Roosevelt quietly slipped away to the White House kitchen, where they requested that the chef prepare hamburgers. Mrs. Roosevelt, delighted with the gift Roy had brought to her husband—a pair of silver spurs with the engraving, "To F. D. R. from Roy Rogers"—enthusiastically quizzed her guest about the making of movies and the training of Trigger.

At Republic, the amount of mail for Roy easily surpassed the previous studio record of famed actress Clara Bow. Roy Rogers Fan Clubs were growing in virtually every major city in the United States and several foreign countries; his recordings were turning a handsome profit in the music stores; and Western Publishing's release of a series of Roy Rogers comic books delighted millions of young readers. Negotiations were underway with the Goodyear Tire and Rubber Company to sponsor a network radio show starring Roy. A tour of Canada was in the planning, and he would soon make his debut in the famed Madison Square Garden where, during a nineteen-day appearance, Roy, Trigger, Gabby Hayes, and the Sons of the Pioneers would be responsible for a new attendance record in New York's historic entertainment center.

Trigger, by now sharing star billing with his famed owner, captivated the New York press, running through his seemingly endless string of tricks. Wearing special cushioned shoes, he even entered the lobby of the Dixie Hotel, took a pencil in his mouth, and registered with a big X. It would seem no publicity gimmick was too outlandish when it involved the King of the Cowboys and the Smartest Horse in the Movies.

In the background Art Rush delighted in the success of his client. While he is hesitant to admit it even today, he had accepted no commission for his work on Roy Rogers's behalf for the first year of their association. Now, with attendance records tumbling everywhere Roy appeared, with prosperous recording and radio contracts signed and development of a merchandising campaign well underway, his client was fast becoming a wealthy man. "The studio still wasn't paying him much," Rush says, "and I think if Herb Yates had known how much he was making outside his work for Republic he would probably have had a heart attack. I'm sure when he agreed to let Roy supplement his income with some of the activities I had suggested, he had no idea how popular and successful his star would be."

Still, it was the movie business which provided the foundation of that success and popularity. With superior script writers like Norton Parker and Louis Stevens contributing strong story lines, and with talented Joe Kane doing the directing, the Roy Rogers vehicles maintained quality a far cut above the general B-Western fare.

"Joe Kane," says Roy, "was an outstanding director, but he was from the old school of screamers and hat-stompers. If someone missed their lines he would throw a fit, generally directing his anger at me, whether I was the one responsible or not. For a reason I couldn't understand for a long time, I was his chosen whipping boy. I was pretty easygoing, though, and for sure I made my share of mistakes, so I usually didn't get upset. But everyone has a limit.

"One afternoon he stopped everything right in the middle of a scene and went into a rage. 'Roy,' he said, 'it's "get," not "git." It seems to me any idiot could get a simple word like that right. If you can't get it right, maybe I should see about getting somebody who can.'

"I told him where I came from it was 'git' and that was the only way I knew how to say it. And if that didn't suit him, maybe he should find another cowboy. And with that I pulled the ultimate Hollywood spoiled-brat stunt and walked off the set for the rest of the day.

"It wasn't one of my prouder moments, but I will have to say that he never yelled at me again. In fact, one day when we were driving out to a location, he apologized and told me he really did like me and hoped I liked him. He began telling me his whole life story, pointing out that he had been short-tempered all his life. 'When I get frustrated,' he said, 'I have to take it out on somebody, and you're the only one I feel I can get away with it on. You aren't the temperamental kind of actor who goes around pouting if you aren't treated with kid gloves, and, believe it or not, I respect you for that.'

"He was one of those people who really didn't mean to harm others, but because of that temper—which I suppose goes along with genius—did. Like I said, I had high regard for him as a director. But it's a wonder I didn't wind up a jibbering idiot during those forty or fifty films we did together."

While the great majority of the B-Westerns never strayed from the Good-Guy-versus-Bad-Guy story line, the Rogers productions generally fell into three categories. Some, like the 1943 production, King of the Cowboys, stressed two-fisted, hard-riding action with stuntmen providing breathtaking tricks of physical skill. In that picture, for instance, famed stuntman Yak Canutt performed a stunt which would be copied by Western filmmakers for years to come—letting a wagon pass over him, grabbing the back of it and hoisting himself in.

Then there would be those pictures which stressed plot and music. Third was the speedy story line which wasted little time leading up to a wild and exciting action wind-up with fistfights, chase scenes, and an occasional shoot-out. In this, the most common type of the Roy Rogers films, wrong would be righted with time left over to allow Roy and friends to provide the audiences with a five-or-ten-minute musical revue. The fans not only left the theater houses satisfied they had seen the action they had come to expect, but were also humming a tune.

As Roy Rogers's value to the studio grew with each picture, his involvement in the more dangerous scenes lessened, turned over to more expendable stuntmen. Trainer Glenn Randall even managed to convince Roy and studio executives to use a double for Trigger on occasion in lengthy chase scenes, explaining that the constant work of the Republic schedule, which called for eight pictures a year, would eventually shorten the screen life of the gifted horse.

"I never got hurt during the filming of a movie, though there was one time when I thought sure Yak Canutt was going to personally see to it that I was. And not without good reason.

"We were doing this close-up, and he was standing in for the 'heavy' in the picture. The scene called for me to deliver this knockout uppercut to his chin. Yak, who was one of the greatest stuntmen of all time and who went on to become a successful director, doing things like the action scenes in Ben Hur, carefully explained to me how I was supposed to deliver the blow. He had this neckerchief that he held out away from his face ever so slightly and I was supposed to bring my fist up under it and he would jerk his head back, making it look as if I had knocked his head off.

"Things didn't quite go as planned, since he wasn't able to judge where my fist was as it came up under the neckerchief. I landed a good shot squarely to his jaw, chipping three or four teeth and actually dazing him a little bit. I felt terrible about it, apologizing as I helped him up.

" 'Don't think anything about it,' Yak said, 'Happens all the time.' Some way to make a living if you ask me."

While the B-Westerns abounded with action and song, there was little room for the development of parts for leading ladies.

They appeared to do little more than look pretty, cast loving looks at the star, maybe sing along on a song or two, and ultimately get saved from whatever tight spot the scriptwriter placed them in.

In addition to the several pictures with Lynn (Mary Hart) Roberts, Roy had a succession of leading ladies, many of them beauty contest winners who had come to Hollywood, signed six-month contracts, and were put into B-Westerns where their acting skills or lack of same were not likely to endure any severe tests. Among those who appeared on the screen with Roy were Sally Payne, Gale Storm, Peggy Moran, Ruth Terry, and Linda Hayes.

And then, in 1944, as shooting of The Cowboy and the Senorita *was about to begin, Roy was told that a young actress who had been working in radio and musical comedies would be working with him.*

Her name, he was told, was Dale Evans.

DALE AND I got along well right from the start.

She did, however, have a little to learn about working in Westerns. Learning that she was originally from Texas, it occurred to me that I might finally have a leading lady who could also ride a horse. But in her first riding scene she bounced along like she was on a merry-go-round. I kidded her about it, pointing out that I couldn't ever remember seeing that much daylight between a horse and rider outside a few rodeos I'd been to, but she failed to see much humor in my observation. She was far more concerned over the fact that the ride had jarred several new caps from her teeth and her horse had stepped all over the four-hundred-dollar smile a studio had just finished paying for.

What she lacked in horsewomanship, though, she more than made up for with her energetic acting and singing. And what the heck; Gabby had been forty-five before he ever learned to ride.

It was Gabby who repeatedly pointed out that better parts were needed for the leading ladies in Westerns. "Half of the people going to see our pictures," he would argue, "are girls. They want to see the ladies involved in the stories more. Maybe even with a little romance. I don't think the theaters are going to empty like somebody's hollered 'Fire!' if Roy was to kiss somebody other than Trigger on the screen. A little hand-holding and peckin' on the cheek would make a lot of little ladies happy."

I have to admit that I seriously questioned tampering with what I figured to be an already-successful, tried-and-proven formula. On the other hand, *Movie Life* magazine had conducted a poll which indicated that the majority of theatergoers did, in fact, want a little romance. That did not escape the attention of the powers-that-be at Republic. In the very next picture I did with Dale, the script called for me to give her a brotherly kiss on the forehead. A long way from being X-rated, you must admit, but there were those die-hards who wondered if B-Westerns would ever be the same. For a while I was one of those die-hards.

Of course, I have to admit that it wasn't my first screen kiss. That had come earlier in a movie entitled *San Fernando Valley,* from little Jean Porter in a dream sequence.

While the kissing and hand-holding never got out of hand, the parts written for Dale rose far above those my previous leading ladies had been dealt. And the public accepted her immediately.

She had made it clear from the beginning that she aspired to act in musicals but, to her credit, she approached her work in our Westerns with a professional dedication that came through loud and clear every time a new picture was released.

And she was a warm, likable woman who didn't mind the hard work, dust, dirt, and horseback riding that went along with her job. Arlene and the girls visited the set regularly and immediately took a strong liking to her as well. Dale's dressing room, in fact, soon became the favorite playground of Cheryl and Linda Lou.

I liked her, too. How could I help it? She was the first leading lady I'd ever had who bothered to take riding lessons.

IN ADDITION to making movies, she also joined us on the road for personal appearances. In short order she found that it in no way resembled the club singing she had done before making her way to California. During one rodeo performance in Detroit, Michigan, her horse spooked and made four wild gallops around the arena before wranglers could stop it and help her off. In Las Vegas, a balcony under which she had been standing just minutes earlier collapsed. And the Baker Hotel where she was staying in Dallas was rocked with an explosion just shortly after she had left. Being a sagebrush sweetheart wasn't easy.

And it was her good fortune, or lack of same, to get into the Western movie business when Republic Studios discovered a whole new and previously untapped market. They decided that if a touch of Spanish accent was added here and a chorus sung in the native tongue of Mexico added there, a whole new market would be opened south of the border. They were right. Duncan Renaldo, who would later gain fame as the Cisco Kid, taught me Spanish, as did Estelita Rodriquez, who joined us for *Along the Navajo Trail.*

In fact, for her first role with me Dale wore a black wig and played the part of Ysobel Martinez. She still had a healthy Texas drawl (which to this day she's never lost) and during the filming of *The Cowboy and the Senorita,* Fuzzy Knight repeatedly warned her not to get her Spanish and her Texican, as he called it, mixed up. "If you don't watch yourself," he would chide, "you'll be saying, 'si si, you all.' "

She made it through the movie with flying colors, however, and returned home to Texas for a short vacation with her family. While attending an ice show in the Century Room of the swank Adolphus Hotel in Dallas, the orchestra leader asked her to do a song. As she was making her way to the bandstand, trying to negotiate the ice in high heels, she did a swan dive which was captured by a photographer.

As soon as the photo made its way out to California I sent her a telegram which said, *It could have been worse. At least this time there was no horse to step on your teeth.*

To this day she's never bothered to tell me whether she found my message funny.

Show business, it seems, has a way of inviting embarrassing moments. One of mine came in 1945. We were in New York, working Madison Square Garden at the same time the New York Yankees and the St. Louis Cardinals were battling it out in the World Series. Since I was eager to see at least one game of the Series, Ned Irish, the president of the Garden, arranged for Art Rush and me to join him in his box seats.

It was a big thrill for me, going out to the ballpark early to visit with people like Connie Mack and Babe Ruth and Judge Kenesaw Mountain Landis, but as soon as we took our seats in Ned Irish's season box, people began coming over and asking for autographs. It didn't bother me until the game was just about to begin and the crowd kept coming. I leaned over to Art Rush and told him that if we weren't able to get these people to return to their seats we'd have to leave, since a lot of people around us weren't going to be able to see the game.

Just as Art was leaving his seat to go speak to the security guards about the problem, I turned to see this man coming—not down the aisle, but climbing over seats, obviously headed in my direction. So intent was he on reaching his destination that he was apparently oblivious to the people he was stepping over and otherwise inconveniencing. Just before he got to my seat he climbed over a box, stumbled slightly, and steadied himself by placing his hand on the hat of a man who had been sitting quietly, puffing on a cigar, waiting for the game to begin.

As soon as I realized who that man was, I immediately began stuttering an apology while Art, aghast over the development, was brushing the man off and trying to smooth his crumpled hat. Former President Herbert Hoover just smiled a warm, patient smile and said, "It's quite all right. No harm done. It so happens that I'm a Roy Rogers fan myself."

Of course with the tight security given the President today, something like that could never occur. I would have enjoyed the game a great deal more had it not occurred on that particular fall afternoon thirty-five years ago.

IT WOULD HAVE BEEN DIFFICULT in the mid-forties to find many people who wouldn't have traded places with Roy Rogers; he had become one of the most famous men in America and around the world. Success seemed to breed more success. Children loved him and parents appreciated him. He was, in the tired idiom of show business, a bonafide star of stage, screen, radio, and juke boxes throughout the land.

He was financially secure, had a loving wife and two daughters who were the lights of his life. And then, as if the American Dream story had no ending, Arlene gave birth to a son on October 28, 1946. News of the arrival of Roy Rogers, Jr., a healthy boy who would come to be known as Dusty, was spread throughout the world by the wire services.

"At that time in my life," Roy remembers, "I couldn't, even in my wildest imagination, think of anything else I would want. I was feeling pretty good about myself, in fact. Cocky is perhaps a better adjective.

"But the Lord has a way of making you aware of how fragile the thing everyone calls success is. He can take a pretty big ego and get it back down to size in a real hurry. I know. I learned it the hard way."

Six days after the birth of his son, Roy had a Sunday morning golf date with Art Rush. So excited had he been over the arrival of Roy, Jr., that production of the movie on which he was working at the time had been shut down for a week—the exciting distraction had made concentrating on his lines all but impossible. A round of golf, Art had suggested earlier, would be good for him—help him burn off some of his excess energy.

Well before he was to meet his golfing partner, however, the phone rang in his home. It was the hospital, urging him and Arlene's mother, who had come to stay and help her daughter with the new baby for a couple of weeks, to hurry to the hospital.

When they reached Arlene's room they found it crowded with stern-faced doctors and nurses. Arlene lay unconscious, the victim of a sudden embolism. Artificial respiration, injections, and oxygen had failed to do any good.

Shortly after her husband arrived, Arlene Rogers died.

It would be Mary Jo Rush who answered the phone later and rushed upstairs to wake her still-sleeping husband. "I don't know who it is on the phone," she told her husband, "but it sounds urgent. It sounded like a child crying to me."

Lifting the receiver, Art Rush heard the sobbing Roy Rogers

say the words that sent a frozen chill through his body. "Art," he heard, "Arlene's dead . . ."

Suddenly Art Rush was also crying. *"Where are you?"*

"The hospital."

"Stay there. I'm on the way."

Art stopped his frantic dressing only long enough to kneel and say a prayer. A deeply religious man, he says, *"I just knew we needed help and I asked for it."* He then hurried to the hospital.

"When I got there I saw something," Rush says, *"that I can still see in my mind as if it were yesterday. There was Roy, standing next to his car in the parking lot, tears in his eyes, and kids surrounding him. He was signing autographs. Crying and signing autographs.*

"I know the grief he was bearing was far greater than mine, but that scene just broke my heart. There he was, his spirit broken, not even trying to hide his tears, but still signing the pieces of paper all those little kids were holding out to him."

Such was the mettle of the King of the Cowboys.

Leonard, Mattie, and Andy Slye — between Ohio and California, 1930.

The Sons of the Pioneers, 1934.

Right: Roy Rogers, Republic Studio's new "Singing Cowboy." *Below:* Roy shakes hands with Sol. C. Siegel, his associate producer, immediately after signing a long-term contract with the studio on October 13, 1937.

King of the Cowboys. *Above,* moving clockwise: *Springtime in the Sierras* (1947), *Jesse James at Bay* (1941), *Utah* (1945). *Below:* With Gabby Hayes in *Days of Jesse James* (1939).

Queen of the West. *Above, top:* Making a picture in the early 1940s. *Above, center:* Learning to stay on a rearing horse. *Right:* On location, late 1944.

Opposite page: Together on location, 1945.

Roy's and Dale's wedding at the Flying L Ranch, Davis, Oklahoma, on December 31, 1947. Left: Roy and Dale with Rev. Bill Alexander. *Below:* With Art and Mary Jo Rush, Roy's and Dale's Best Man and Matron of Honor.

Family Portraits. *Above:* Roy and Dale with Dale's family at their wedding. From left to right, they are Aunt Estelle Bell; brother Hillman Smith; Dale's mother, Mrs. Walter Hillman Smith; Aunt Annie Merle Pulliam; Dale's father, Walter Hillman Smith; Roy; son Tom Fox; and Dale.

Below: Roy and Dale with Roy's parents and sisters at Shy Haven Ranch, Lake Hughes, California. Cleda is seated on sofa; Kathleen and Mary are standing.

The day after the wedding —
New Year's Day at the
Flying L Ranch.

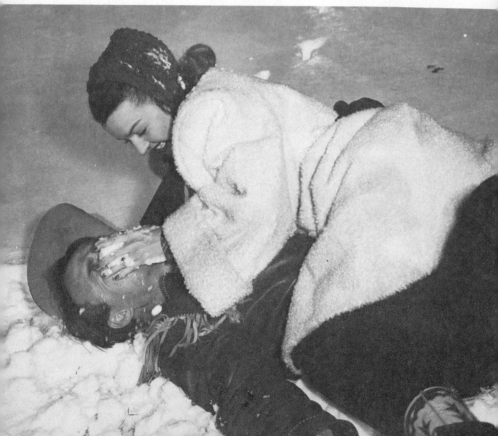

Part Two

Queen of the West

*I*t sits quietly on the southern edge of Ellis County in central Texas, claiming 1,309 residents, a downtown area which has seen better days, and an economy destined to rise and fall in direct proportion to the annual amount of rainfall.

Less than an hour's drive from the high-geared, high-finance world of Dallas, little Italy, Texas, is a farming community struggling to survive and maintain its traditions in a time when rural traditions are daily being swept away by what legislators and congressmen are wont to call progress. In that regard, Italy and her people hold stubbornly to old and time-tested values. The pace is slow and the living, if not luxurious, is easy, without the yoke of big-city pressures. In Italy, people don't expend great amounts of effort keeping up with the Joneses. They're too busy working the fields, going to church, helping their neighbors, and minding their own business.

On this particular day, however, the pace was noticeably quicker, the enthusiasm obvious on the face of virtually every man, woman, and child. By careful design it was not meant to be an average day in Italy. Red, white, and blue bunting draped the town; taped music, fed into a loudspeaker system, filled the square, causing the regular patrons of the sidewalk benches to tap their feet as they attended their whittling ritual.

On one corner a popcorn vendor was set up for business, much to the delight of his youthful clientele, and energetic young members of the Chamber of Commerce were busily roping off a block of Main Street which would, when evening fell, serve as an open-air square dance floor. Byer's Ladies Shop, in celebration of the occasion, was offering blouses three for ten dollars; The Pink Elephant Variety Store had followed *suit and was doing a brisk business with its own Homecoming Sale. Soon, however, their doors would close, so that owners and salespersons would be allowed proper time to prepare for the much-anticipated activities to come.*

The most famous citizen ever to call their town home had returned to take a bow at their own request. Not that she hadn't been back often over the years to visit her parents and rekindle old friendships. This time, however, there was to be pomp and circumstance, with a Key to the City and a plaque and a stage constructed from bales of hay and a flatbed truck. First class in every respect.

This, a Chamber of Commerce brainchild, was to be the official Dale Evans Homecoming.

So what if for years Waxahachie, just a few minute's drive up Interstate 35, had boasted long and loud that Mary Martin, the gifted actress who brought Peter Pan *to life on the Broadway stage, was one of its own? Had Ms. Martin returned so much as to say hello? No, and in fact, she had more than once publicly discredited her birthplace as, for starters, backward and boring.*

Not so with Dale Evans, the Queen of the West. She had remained as loyal and loving to her hometown as it had to her. A Dale Evans Day was clearly in order.

People came, not just from Italy, but from such surrounding hamlets as Avalon, Milford, and Lone Cedar to shake her hand, to hear her sing, and to praise the work she had done both as an entertainer and a humanitarian. Many of the adults recalled particular Saturday afternoons when they sat in darkened movie houses to watch Dale and Roy go about winning the West with a song in their hearts. Youngsters, familiar with Dale Evans only through the memories of their parents, stood patiently to have their pictures taken with the lady of the hour and have her sign her name to autograph books and scraps of paper.

"There's a feeling in a little town like this," Dale told the crowd, "that is vanishing all too fast in America. Here, people care about each other."

Dale Evans Day stood as eloquent testimony to her observation.

6

FOR AS LONG AS I CAN REMEMBER I've been hearing and reading about people who are "trying to find out who they are." They think *they've* had problems. Consider this:

Until not too many years ago the only evidence I had of my birth was an affidavit from my parents assuring any and all who cared to know that I was born Frances Octavia Smith on October 31, 1912, in the home of my grandparents in Uvalde, Texas. That was good enough for me, and the people down at the driver's license bureau and the passport authorities and the man down at the grocery store who cashes checks for me.

But in 1954, when Roy and I were preparing to travel to England, I was unable to find the affidavit. I immediately wrote to the Bureau of Vital Statistics in Texas to finally request a copy of my birth certificate. It came back with the surprising news that I had been born on October 30 instead of October 31, and that my name was Lucille Wood Smith. Take your choice.

My mother, who was the only lady I ever knew who could call someone a card-carrying crazy and do so in a Christian manner, later insisted to me that the record-keepers in Texas were obviously not to be considered reliable and that there was absolutely no question in her mind that I was named Frances Octavia. I figure a mother should know better than a dusty old file cabinet, so, for the record, Frances Octavia Smith it will be. As far as the birthdate goes, my mother admitted she wasn't sure. Since I'd spent a great deal of my adult life dealing with jokes about being born on Halloween, I've stuck with October 31, despite the fact that it makes me a day older. Or is it younger? No matter; I figure when you get my age it really doesn't matter anyway. I just go along and, with the help of God and a little Max Factor, try to look the best I can.

Which, to be truthful, isn't nearly as important to me today as it was at one time in my life.

I HAVE NO STORIES of childhood poverty to tell. While my father was by no means a wealthy man, he fell into that comfortable middle-class range as a farmer and owner-operator of his own hardware store during my younger days. I always had a new Easter dress, and was given piano lessons, an allowance and, quite honestly, what amounted to an improper amount of attention inasmuch as I was the first child born to Walter and Betty Sue Smith.

Although my parents farmed near Italy, Texas, I was born in my grandfather's home in Uvalde—the home town of former Vice-President John Nance Garner and actor Dana Andrews, as well as the infamous Newton Gang, a collection of brothers who gained nationwide fame—and fortune—by pulling off a record-setting million-dollar train robbery near Chicago in the early twenties.

If that doesn't legitimately qualify it as a social melting pot, I don't use the same yardstick you do.

It was I who, at the roaring age of three, decided one Sunday morning that all gathered at our little Italy Baptist church would be witness to my gospel solo debut. I swished my skirt down the aisle, burst into song, and would later be rewarded by a trip with my father to the nearby fire station, where he made every effort to convince me he was a firm believer in the "spare the rod, spoil the child" school of thought. I got the same message when, upon coming to the realization that the birth of my younger brother Hillman was a major distraction from me, I ran away from home—all the way to the pig pen out back where, in mud up to my Dutch bob, I told my woeful tale to a newly born litter of pigs.

We moved to Osceola, Arkansas, when I was seven, my father having heeded the call of his brother who told him stories of wonder about the bountiful cotton crops a man could raise there. He had failed to mention the occasional floods which broke down levees, turning roads and cotton fields alike into seas of mud, or of how crop-killing boll weevils flourished and mosquitoes sometimes darkened the late evening sky.

The first year was neither financially rewarding nor joyous to the Smith family, but my father, a hard worker who wasn't the least bit hesitant about butting heads with challenges, saw to it that the next year was more productive.

Having already been taught the basics of reading, writing, and math by my mother, I entered school at age seven. After half a year in the first grade, I was advanced all the way to the third. I would later also skip the seventh, thus arriving at the eighth grade at the ripe age of eleven. And I promptly had a nervous breakdown which made it necessary to spend an entire summer vacation in bed.

Trying to keep up with a group of kids several years my senior, I had pushed myself too hard. I was, Mother would remind me years later, a child who never went about any activity at a normal speed. For me it was full throttle or not at all.

Which was the main reason my piano instructor finally came to the end of her patience and left our home one afternoon in the middle of a lesson. "Mrs. Smith," she said before leaving, "I'm wasting my time and your money. Your daughter is too much of an improviser to ever learn to play properly. She won't practice the scales or the pieces I assign to her."

The routine tedium of running up and down the scales didn't appeal to me in the least, so I had spent my practice time improvising my own compositions. Even with the lack of an instructor (aside from the help my mother would give me), I continued to play, learning by ear the kinds of songs I could also sing. Which is exactly where my musical abilities are today.

As a youngster, I spent a great deal of time impulsively rushing into things long before I was emotionally ready to deal with them. I regularly attended church with my parents, but my motives were more social than spiritual. It wasn't until our church held its annual revival, inviting a guest preacher

whose hell-fire and brimstone sermons got my attention, that
I gave religion any serious thought. Having decided I did not
wish to spend my eternity in either the darkness or the fire
he so eloquently described, I walked the aisle and was baptized
a couple of weeks later. I was ten at the time, reaching out
in fear but not really prepared to dedicate, to hand my life
over to the Lord.

By the time I was twelve and a freshman in high school, I
was anxious to participate in all the activities my generally-
older classmates were enjoying—the parties and the public
dances held on weekends at the courthouse. Without question,
the most fascinating discovery I had made up to that time
was boys. I looked older than I was, acted older—certainly
felt older—and therefore was regularly distraught when Mother
wouldn't readily allow me to accept the offers of dates which
came with enough frequency to keep my already healthy ego
properly inflated.

Will, however, finds a way, and I finally succeeded in persuading my mother to attend the dances as a chaperon. Soon I
was dancing every dance.

It was at one of those weekly dances a couple of years
later that I met an older boy from a nearby town and fell
head over heels in love. In his late teens, he was handsome,
fun-loving, and was soon telling me that he loved me. Now
that I was allowed to date, we went everywhere together. He
became the focal point of my whole life, a state of affairs
which greatly concerned my mother. First, she suggested we
see a little less of each other. I ignored her. Finally, in desperation, she told me I was not to see him anymore. I did anyway.
I was, after all, fourteen years old, and quite capable of making
decisions on my own. If my romance had to become a sneak-
around affair, so be it.

One evening I was supposed to attend a school play rehearsal
and then go on over to a girlfriend's house to spend the night.
It was the last my mother would hear of me for three days.

Lying about our ages, my boyfriend had obtained a marriage
license. On the evening I was supposed to be practicing for
my role in the play, we drove eighteen miles down the road
to Blytheville, where we were married in the home of a local

minister. Then we drove on across the border to Tennessee, where we spent our honeymoon weekend in the home of my new mother-in-law.

While I had no second thoughts about the boy I had married, concern over the grief I knew I had caused my parents gnawed at me. Knowing that Mother would be frantic, I called her long distance to announce that Frances Smith was now officially Mrs. Frances Fox.

The silence that followed was deafening.

Once the shock had passed Mother asked that we come back to Osceola so that I could at least finish high school, a suggestion I unfortunately rejected. We returned home, living with my husband's father and step-mother.

I would soon share in my parents' disappointment at my new life. Or at least experience disappointments of my own. Twice in the first six months of our marriage my husband left me. When my parents decided to move to Memphis I went with them, hoping my new husband would soon follow.

He was there when, at age fifteen, I gave birth to our son, but shortly thereafter he left for the third and final time. All of my things and the baby's things had been left in my aunt's and uncle's garage, and in a few long days came the final communication from the boy I had planned to spend my life with. A letter arrived, talking of a need for freedom, of being too young to be tied down to a wife and a child. I was heartbroken.

Another year would pass before I could bring myself to file for divorce. At age seventeen, a bitter divorcee, I found myself running everywhere and getting nowhere. Totally disillusioned, I struck out in all directions, literally daring anyone to knock the sizable chip from my shoulder. All I succeeded in doing was hurting myself and others, never realizing what an emotionally immature and insecure—and selfish—person I was. In a way that really made no sense, I was trying to rationalize my feelings of guilt and failure, to justify my wrongdoing.

I declared independence against the world. Mother, quietly aware of the darkness I was walking in, offered to adopt my child. I wouldn't even consider it. There would be, henceforth, only one man in my life that I would trust. Tommy Fox was my son, I loved him dearly, and it would be I who took care of him.

To properly do so, I realized, I had to find a job. Because of my high grades in high school a Memphis business school allowed me to enroll without benefit of a diploma. Somehow, somewhere, I would find my success and build a life for my young son and me. Despite the scars, I was still a dreamer; certain castles could be built thereon.

The typing and shorthand I learned in business school would, I felt, hold me in good stead, but my aspirations leaned more toward the creative. I could write short stories, sell them to magazines, and thereby never have need for leaving my son to the care of others. As a fiction writer I was a thundering failure, receiving nothing but rejection slips for my efforts.

I tried song writing. Considering myself a reasonably objective judge, I tossed my first several efforts where they belonged. But once having written one I was pleased with, I took it personally to a Memphis music publisher and sang it to him. It had possibilities, he told me; leave it and he would get back to me with some kind of decision. That decision was evidently never made, since I've yet to get his call. I have to point out, though, that several months later, in a record store, I heard a song which, except for a few slight alterations and the name of another composer affixed to it, was the one I had sung. Score another point for experience.

I decided to limit my creative efforts to the singing I had begun doing in church, and took a job with a bus company for twelve dollars a week. That lasted three weeks. I left the day an insurance company offered me a secretarial job at better wages. My salary would be fifteen dollars a week.

I have to admit that I wasn't the most devoted accident report typist they ever had. Few aspiring songwriters, I imagine, would be. One afternoon while my boss was out of the office I set my work aside and tried to work on a song I had been writing, singing to myself as I went. The song died with the slamming of the door and my employer suggesting that perhaps I was in the wrong business. Certain that I was very shortly going to be picking up my paycheck, I wondered if the position with the bus company was still open.

Instead, my boss complimented me on my singing and asked if I would be interested in singing on a radio show which the company sponsored on a small local station. That next Friday night, with visions of grandeur dancing in her head, Frances Fox made her radio singing debut, doing a song titled "Mighty Lak a Rose." Of course there was no pay involved, but that didn't matter.

In those days you were permitted to dedicate your songs to anyone you wished. My first dedication was to my son Tommy.

WHEN THE STATION asked me if I would become a regular on the thirty-minute request program, I was certain I was on my way. I worked at the insurance office by day and prepared for my career as the songbird of the South by night. Soon I was being invited to entertain at civic luncheons, banquets, and occasional parties. Generally the pay was a meal and a handshake, but occasionally I would receive five or ten dollars which would make a considerable difference in the Fox family budget.

So, too, would the fact that in a few short months I had graduated from the thirty-minute request show on one of Memphis's smallest stations to a show on the largest station in town.

In 1930, live radio was big. Memphis, however, was far from the mainstream. Success as a radio personality was reached only after one had performed on one of the powerful Chicago stations which reached far and deep into the heartland of America.

Four years in Memphis, I felt, was experience enough. So what if the Chicago papers were full of stories about a roaring depression which was putting thousands out of work, that the Charles Lindberghs' baby had been kidnapped, and that the unsavory likes of such as Al Capone and John Dillinger were reportedly roaming the streets. I typed up my last insurance report and Tommy and I headed for the Windy City.

And proceeded to very nearly starve to death. My experience and small successes in Memphis impressed not a single radio station, club manager, or big band in Chicago. Again desperate,

I finally managed to locate another secretarial job, only to find out that fifteen dollars a week in Chicago wouldn't even stretch as far as twelve had in Memphis. Expenses included rent, a fee for a babysitter to watch Tommy when he returned from school, coats to protect us from a chill factor we had never before known, and food. All too many times, there was precious little of the latter in the house.

For almost two years I beat my head against that wall—still stubborn, still ambitious to a fault, still holding my grudge against the world like a shield. Even though it frustrated me to admit it, I was getting tired and more lonely than I had ever been.

One cold morning as I bundled Tommy up to send him off to school, thinking of him going his way, me mine, and neither of us really having anyone else in our lives but each other, it occurred to me how really alone we were.

I had been to see a doctor earlier. After examining me, he told me I was suffering from acute malnutrition. Enough was enough.

Setting my so-carefully-guarded pride aside for a moment, I wired Mother and Dad, who had by then also left Memphis in favor of a farm back in Italy. We needed money, the wire said, to come home.

A few days in the hospital, a lot of good home cooking and bed rest, and I was feeling like a new person, ready to get back into the fray which had, at times, looked like a titanic battle against so many windmills.

Not long after, I obtained a job at radio station WHAS in Louisville, Kentucky as a female vocalist on the staff. Mother, by now resigned to the fact that her daughter was intent on chasing rainbows, wished me well and suggested that Tommy stay there on the farm with her and Dad and my younger brother Hillman. Despite the fact that Tommy loved the farm and the attention of his grandparents, I refused her offer. I wanted him with me.

The program director at the Louisville station gave me two things upon my arrival—the first well-paying job I had ever had, and a new name. Dale Evans, he said, would be easy for the announcers to say, and was almost impossible to mispronounce or misspell. It suited me. In fact, I was more than a little thrilled over the idea of having a stage name. It went with the business as I understood it, was one of the games the real professionals played. To me it was a sign that I was headed in the right direction.

For the first time in a long time all was well. The good times would not last long, however.

One afternoon as I returned home from work, the lady who had been staying with Tommy told me he had been vomiting all day. Later in the evening he began to complain of pains in his arms and legs. A rush of fear shot through me, because an outbreak of polio in the area was reaching epidemic proportions.

I rushed my son to the hospital, praying to God all the way that he had not contracted the dreaded crippling disease. Frantic, I prayed prayers filled with rash promises as the doctor examined Tommy. "Lord," I said, "If you will see to it that those tests turn out negative, I'll do anything you want me to do. I'll forget about show business. I'll read my Bible every day and I'll pray and be faithful to you. I promise to put you first in my life."

Even to this day I am thrilled to say that the tests turned out negative. I'm ashamed to say, on the other hand, that all those wonderful promises I made in my agonizing hour of need lasted for about two weeks.

The threat of serious illness to my son had frightened me, though, making me even more aware of how much I cared for him. Shortly afterwards, I heard the bad news that the child of a friend of mine had been seriously burned in a home accident while his mother was away at work. I was unable to put it out of my mind. The same thing, I kept hearing myself reminded, could happen to my son.

And there was still the threat of the polio epidemic, which caused me constant fear. It was, I finally decided, not a proper place for a growing boy.

Soon we were on the train, heading back to Texas and the clean, healthy air of the cotton farm.

How Tommy loved that farm, with its wide-open spaces and chickens to chase and rocks to throw, and warm, friendly townspeople to get to know. In short order he was the picture of health.

I began searching for a job a little closer to home. With neither an abundance of jobs for singers nor much need for secretaries in a tiny farming community, I traveled to Dallas where I obtained a job as singer on WFAA's Early Bird program.

I finally agreed to one of my mother's suggestions, allowing Tommy to stay in Italy while I lived in Dallas, returning to the farm on the weekends.

Big changes, it seemed, were finally taking place. I had a good job, Tommy and I were both healthy and happy, and it was good to be back near my parents and Hillman. There were, however, even bigger changes to come.

Robert Dale Butts, a pianist and orchestra leader I had dated occasionally while living in Louisville, called to tell me he was leaving his job with plans to make his way to California. He had thought perhaps he might see what the job possibilities were for a man of his talents in Dallas on the way. If something worked out and he stayed for a while, he said, would I be interested in seeing him?

Of course I would, I told him.

He wound up playing the piano and serving as arranger for WFAA, and I wound up doing something I had never thought I would do again. After we had dated regularly for a year, I married him in the late 1930s.

We decided to move to Chicago to try to further our careers. If first you don't succeed, and all that . . .

We started looking for jobs. After a year, R. Dale landed a job as a composer-arranger at NBC. I registered with a number of booking agencies and began auditioning constantly. The economy of Chicago was in much better shape than it had been on my last visit, and soon I was invited to join the Jay Mills Orchestra, which played regularly at the Edgewater Beach Hotel. It wasn't, to be certain, one of those instant stardom stories. I was very much second string, in fact, since another female singer handled all the soft ballads which were obviously favored by the majority of the ballroom clientele, and I was limited to strictly jazz numbers.

At least I was getting noticed, however, and to my delight

I was asked to audition for the job of lead vocalist with the Anson Weeks Orchestra which was playing the Aragon Ballroom at the time. I was hired, and for the next year toured the country; we did one-night stands in every city in the Midwest and on the West Coast you can name and some you probably can't.

Twelve months and thousands of miles later, I was ready to go home, kick off my shoes, and spend more than an occasional day here and there with my son and husband. A job opened on the staff of a Chicago station and it was given to me.

The fact that I was no longer on the road by no means meant that I was entertaining any thoughts of slowing my work pace. That brass ring was now in view, and I was still chasing it with an obsessive vengeance. I worked for the Chicago-based CBS station by day and in supper clubs by night. My stages were in the Blackstone, Sherman, and Drake hotels, even in the fabled Chez Paree Supper Club.

My debut at the latter was, to put it mildly, a disaster.

Ray Bolger and Ethel Shutta were headlining the show, bringing down the house nightly while I could count on one hand the number of people in the audience who were applauding my efforts. I was crushed.

Then one evening after our last show, Ray and Ethel came into my dressing room for a heart-to-heart talk. Bolger, as straight-talking as he is funny, said, "Dale, you've got a great voice, but your material is working against you. You've got to have some songs that will get the people's attention, make them stop and listen. Maybe some original stuff would help. Do you have a writer?"

I admitted that I had written some songs myself but had never done any of them on the stage. He suggested an impromptu audition there in the dressing room.

A couple of nights later I introduced my "Will You Marry Me, Mr. Laramie?" a novelty tune I had written to commemorate the fact that it was Leap Year, with Ray Bolger playing the role of a stooge as I sang. The audience loved it.

I also worked with people like Fran Allison, who would rise to great fame as part of the Kukla, Fran, and Ollie team;

I even did a recording session with a group of western singers who, for reasons which interested me not in the least, called themselves the Sons of the Pioneers.

Then, just to be sure I had all the bases properly covered, I began doing another show for a local station called "That Gal from Texas." My husband's schedule was equally hectic— we were both very career-oriented, as you've no doubt by now realized. Thus there would be days on end when we would have a chance only to say "hello" and "good-bye" as we passed enroute to our own individual pursuits.

Tommy was ready to enter junior high school, growing into a fine young man. I spent as much time with him as my crazy schedule would allow, making sure that we attended church regularly. I wanted everything for him, including a solid foundation of Christianity and faith. It was, alas, something I had yet to realize I needed for myself as well as my son.

All in all, I thought, I was progressing quite nicely. The money I was earning would enable Tommy to attend a fine college when the time came; my career was expanding to a point where I was enjoying at least some degree of fame. The little ol' country gal from Texas wasn't doing badly at all and was feeling pretty satisfied.

And then, out of the blue, came a call from Hollywood.

7

THERE WERE TIMES when I dreamed of one day advancing to doing musical comedy on the Broadway stage, but Hollywood and the movies had never entered my mind.

Then a wire arrived signed by an agent named Joe Rivkin, explaining that he had heard me on the radio, liked my voice, and suggested I send some photographs of myself. I found the whole thing amusing. This five-foot-two, hundred-and-twenty-something pound, green-eyed, auburn-haired twenty-eight-year-old didn't exactly have to wear a grocery bag over her head when appearing in public, but didn't, to her way of thinking, have the classic looks of the next Harlow or Garbo. I had a good laugh over the whole deal and forgot about it.

Then a second wire came: *Paramount is looking for a new face for female lead in "Holiday Inn." Bing Crosby and Fred Astaire to star.* I showed it to the program director at the radio station, assuming he would find it as amusing as I did. "What do you have to lose?" he said. "Send the guys the pictures; see what happens."

What I figured would happen was that he would take one look at the pictures I had borrowed from our publicity department and decide not to waste any more money on telegrams. Three weeks later, however, yet another wire arrived. It said, *Come at once.*

Like the man said, what did I have to lose? It was a long shot, a fantasy which would doubtless be short-lived, but after talking it over with my husband and Tommy I boarded a plane for my first cross-country trip by air. I arrived looking and feeling more like Hilda the Witch than Dale Evans, Starlet-to-Be. No sooner had the plane left the ground than I developed a throbbing earache. A charter member of the white knuckles flying set, I didn't sleep a wink. Long before we landed in Los Angeles I was thoroughly convinced the whole trip was a bad mistake.

Joe Rivkin, waiting for me when I arrived, would no doubt have agreed. Though in years to come we would develop a strong friendship, we got off to a shaky start.

"Are *you* Dale Evans?" he asked, the tone of his voice making it quite clear that he was hoping to high heaven I wasn't. Having told him that, yes, I was, his facial expression didn't change a bit. "Well," he finally said, "you sure don't look like your pictures." So there I was in Hollywood—nerves, nausea, earache, lack of sleep, and all—wishing very much that I was anywhere else on the globe. Joe Rivkin, no doubt, was feeling the same.

As he drove me to the Hollywood Plaza where I would be staying, he went over my appearance like a man judging a livestock show. He didn't like the lipstick I was wearing; neither the color nor the style of my hair suited him; and the sight of a wedding band on my finger almost caused him to run off the road. "How old are you?" he finally asked.

"Twenty-two," I lied with great bravery.

"As of right now," he replied, "you're twenty-one . . . and single. Understand?"

The games were beginning.

Once at the hotel, he ushered me hurriedly to the beauty salon, advised the operator of the direness of the situation and gave specific instructions on what he wanted done to me in the time remaining before we were to be at Paramount Studios. I felt fortunate at that point that the hotel lobby did not include the office of a plastic surgeon.

With a lighter shade of lipstick, hair tinted and hanging freely, and enough make-up on to hide seven years of age, I finally met Joe in the lobby. The trauma of the trip behind me, I was feeling somewhat better, and was stylishly dressed in a dark dress, white gloves, and the only fur I owned.

"Who died?" Joe asked. At that moment I was thinking how grand it would be if it had been him.

"In Chicago," I testily notified him, "this is considered tasteful dress for a luncheon appointment."

"In Hollywood," he countered, "it is tasteful for funerals and trips to the old folks' home." Obviously, things weren't working out for him. "But never mind, we're already running late."

The scene in the office of the Paramount casting director did little to improve the situation. Joe had given me one of those "let me do the talking" speeches on the way and was, as a matter of fact, doing quite nicely in his sales pitch, until the director asked me if I could dance. Joe quickly fielded the question as he had done most of the other ones: "This girl dances like you wouldn't believe."

That was enough. It was time for me to have a say. "Sir," I said, "I'm a pretty fair ballroom dancer, but that is as far as it goes. Frankly, I can't even do a time step." In the vernacular of the day, that ripped it.

If looks could have killed, the one the casting director dealt Joe Rivkin would have cast an even darker pall over the conversation.

While my career as the female lead alongside Bing Crosby and Fred Astaire ended before it ever got beyond the talking stage, it was finally decided that I should stay on and take a screen test anyway. They made it sound like a salvage job, but I agreed and was told I would do a scene from *Blue Angel* with MacDonald Carey playing opposite me. That brightened the spirits of my new agent.

But I dampened them again shortly thereafter. In a sudden attack of honesty I told him there were a few things he ought to know before the lark went any farther. "Look," I said, "the truth of the matter is I'm twenty-eight years old, not twenty-one or twenty-two. And I have a twelve-year-old son who lives with me."

I thought he was going to be ill. After several minutes of silence he suggested sending Tommy away to school. I wasn't buying. More silence. "If things work out and you are signed to a contract," he pleaded, "this could be very important for you, so I want you to consider it carefully before you answer. You're very young to have a son that old, right? So bring him out here with you and we'll pass him off as your little brother."

The idea was absurd. Hollywood was absurd. The thought of my being offered a contract by Paramount was absurd. So naturally I said, "Okay, I'll go along with it if Tommy will."

For my screen test, Edith Head of the wardrobe department fitted me out with a dress she had created for Barbara Stanwyck, and I played the scene as nearly as the studio drama coach had told me to during our week of sessions. Then I sang a couple of songs on camera, my "Will You Marry Me, Mr. Laramie?" and "I Don't Know Why I Love You Like I Do," and was done with it. I was quite ready to get back to Chicago and on with my career.

It would be three weeks before I heard from Joe. Once again, his opening remarks were far from flattering. Paramount's scouting report had read something like this: good voice, no dancing ability, needs to lose some weight. In view of the fact Joe Rivkin had seen to it that I lost twelve pounds during the time I was on the West Coast preparing for the screen test, I did a slow boil. "Mr. Rivkin," I said, "I didn't care for your movie business any more than it evidently cared for me, so I guess we're about even. Thank you very much for calling."

As I was preparing to hang up, he literally yelled into the phone. "There's more," he said, "I've got something else to tell you. Paramount isn't interested, but Twentieth Century-Fox has seen your screen test and is ready to sign you to a one-year contract."

The news, which he no doubt thought glorious, drew no response from me. When no reply was forthcoming, he opted to fill the silence himself. "Dale, they're willing to pay you four hundred dollars a week. That's got to be about three times what you're making singing there in Chicago."

Who says agents don't tell the truth? He had his figures almost to the penny. I told him I'd think about it and get back to him.

Suddenly Hollywood seemed to offer a lot of possibilities. In addition to the salary they were offering me at Twentieth Century-Fox, a move to California might also afford my husband the opportunity to realize a dream of his own. For a composer-arranger there was no place better to be than in Hollywood.

The hard part was trying to explain to a twelve-year-old boy whom I had tried very hard to teach honesty that it would be necessary for his mother to tell people he was actually her younger brother. "It sounds silly to me," he said, "but you can do it if you want to. I will not lie about it myself; I am a Christian"—and he was.

I called Mother to tell her the news, and suggested she accompany Tommy and me to California while we searched for an apartment and settle in. Leaving my husband behind to finish out his contract with the station in Chicago, I was back on the plane, white knuckles and all, headed West to goodness knows what.

My mother brought along only one word of instruction from Dad back on the farm. "He said for me to tell you," she reported, "not to let anybody kiss you on the screen and don't show your legs."

IF ANYONE had wanted to kiss me on the screen during my tenure with Twentieth Century, he would have had to do so in one big hurry. I had a grand total of two walk-ons, neither of which demanded great acting ability.

Shortly after I arrived, it looked as if my career was going to get off with a bang once I was past the traditional preparatory ritual of being shuttled off to a health studio to lose another pound or two, getting a tooth here and there capped, and paying frequent visits to the studio dramatic coach. And of course there was a need to take yet another screen test.

Finally, however, it was announced that my road to stardom would begin with a college musical to be entitled *Campus in the Clouds*. World War II shot it right out of the sky. When the war broke out, just a few weeks before we were to go into production, the Twentieth Century executives decided to scrap the picture. They determined that it was not a proper time in American history to try to sell the public on the idea that college life was carefree and full of song. I had to agree with their decision, but was by no means pleased with it. That, I'm afraid to say, was how Dale Evans was in those days. What right did World War II have starting up just at the time I was preparing to take the motion picture business by storm?

Executives at the studio told me not to worry, that they would soon have something else for me. They did—everything you could imagine but doing movies. I took some dance lessons and was placed under the tutelage of a very elegant and famous British voice coach named Flossie Friedman. By the time we were finished she must have known very well how my piano teacher back in Osceola felt. The first reading she had me do, Rudyard Kipling's poem "If," sent her into a mild shock. I can still hear her voice, saying, "My dah-ling, you must be kidding. That accent is absolutely horrible. I'm afraid we shall never be able to eradicate it." She was one hundred percent right. Even today it's alive and doing quite well, thank you.

While I was admittedly disappointed with the fact that I was doing precious little movie work, I was doing a great deal of singing, traveling around to the various training camps to entertain. My brother Hillman was, at the time, in the Air Corps, and it didn't take me long to outrank him, since the Air Force had made me an honorary captain for my entertaining efforts. I was also recording a lot of songs that were being shipped overseas.

In all, I think I did something like six hundred shows for the USO and the Hollywood Victory Committee. R. Dale accompanied me on as many of my trips as his schedule would permit, playing piano for me. We were on the go so much, in fact, that it didn't seem like we ever had much chance to properly convert the Spanish-style house in which we were living into a real home.

But I was learning a great deal which I was certain would serve me well whenever—if ever—my time came to do the work in movies I had been hired to do.

While I wasn't on the screen, I was working alongside some of Hollywood's biggest names at the military training camps, marveling at the professional manner in which they approached performances in settings far removed from sound studios.

Once, I was working with Pat O'Brien and Marlene Dietrich at a camp in northern California. The conditions were the worst you could imagine, yet Miss Dietrich prepared herself as if she were going on stage at the Palace—false eyelashes, slinky black sequin gown, the whole bit. When she and Pat went out there on stage they gave it everything they had. And the soldiers knew it.

That, I think, was the first time I realized the obligation real entertainers feel toward their audience. It was one of the most valuable lessons I've ever learned.

I was beginning to wonder, though, if I was ever going to get the opportunity to put such lessons to use. With my contract having about run its course, I began to get nervous. Complicating matters was the fact that Joe Rivkin, my agent, had entered the Armed Forces in special services and was now stationed at Sheppard Field in Wichita Falls, Texas. When I began to hear the rumors that Twentieth Century-Fox was planning to bid me farewell when my year's contract was up, I called Joe and asked what he thought I should do.

As a matter of fact, I had already taken the situation into my own hands to some degree, quietly doing a screen test for MGM in hopes of landing a part in a Kay Kyser film they were planning, but nothing had come of it.

Once again it was sinking in on me that I belonged on radio, so I asked Joe if he could recommend a Los Angeles agent who could be of help to me in that field. If I wanted to see another movie, I could buy a ticket.

The man he recommended was Art Rush, who—wouldn't you know it—had never had a female client in his life. Still, after I had contacted him, he agreed to come by the house one evening and listen to me sing. Bringing along his wife Mary Jo, herself once an actress, he listened and, to my good fortune, liked what he heard. "I have to admit to you," he told me later, "that I did not arrive at your house with a great deal of optimism. But I like the way you sing. So does Mary Jo. I'll see what I can do about setting up a radio audition."

The news did not come too soon. Without notice, I officially became history to Twentieth Century-Fox as soon as my contract expired.

To this day I am amazed at the success Art Rush has enjoyed in the business. A soft-spoken, gentle man of strong Christian persuasion, there is not the slightest trace of hard-sell apparent in his manner. Yet his track record spoke for itself. It had, in fact, been Joe who told me that Art was the only other agent he would recommend because of his unquestioned honesty. That, in retrospect, was one of the biggest things Art Rush had—and still has—going for him.

In short order he called to tell me of an audition he had arranged. NBC's "Chase and Sanborn Hour," starring Edgar Bergen and Charley McCarthy, as well as Don Ameche and Ray Noble, was in need of a female vocalist.

I knew I had the job the minute that crazy puppet Charley McCarthy began whistling through his wooden mouth. I smiled, Edgar Bergen smiled, Art Rush smiled. A few days later I signed a contract.

PROFESSIONALLY SPEAKING, I was again doing well. Personally, however, I was struggling with some big problems.

For starters, I was sick of living the lie about my son. It was an absurd thing I was being a party to—and forcing him to be a party to as well. We never discussed the matter, but I knew that deep down he was unhappy about the role he was being forced to play. When, for instance, the studio had sent out photographers to do some pictures of me at home,

Tommy quietly disappeared, almost as if on cue. Once I was invited to a Christmas party to which everyone was to bring their children. I took Tommy with me, but introduced him around as my brother. Sitting in the stands at a football game, watching him perform as a member of the school band at halftime, I wanted so badly to tell someone, anyone, that my son was out there playing the flute, that I could have screamed.

All I did was remain silent. And I hated every minute of it.

Tommy was also enthusiastically involved in the church, getting spiritually stronger with every passing day. We attended the Hollywood First Baptist Church regularly, and the sermons had begun to cause me great concern. On one particular Sunday morning the minister, Dr. Harold Proppe, spoke of those people with God-given musical talent who refused to honor the Lord by putting those gifts to use in the church. I felt his remarks were aimed directly at me, as if there were no one else in the congregation.

Following the service Tommy looked at me with those searching eyes of his. He said nothing but, it occurred to me, he knew a lot.

I WAS FINDING OUT a few things that I hadn't previously known about as well. Like, for instance, the power wielded by executives of major radio networks and ad agencies. On two different occasions one such executive connected with the "Chase and Sanborn Hour" in New York asked me to have dinner with him. Both times I declined because of prior engagements. And in the fall of 1943 my option was not renewed.

I was in search of a job, and once again my agent was out of pocket. From the first time I met Art Rush he had regularly told me of the successes and promising future of a singing cowboy client of his. Quite obviously proud of this man named Roy Rogers, Art seemed unable to carry on a conversation of any duration without mention of his name. When I was singing at Edwards Air Force Base in Lancaster, California, sharing the stage with the Sons of the Pioneers, Art had made it a special point to introduce me to his protégé. No skyrockets went off; no bells rang. Roy Rogers seemed to me to be a rather shy, mannerly cowboy with reasonably good looks and a nice singing voice. Nothing more, nothing less.

The truth of the matter was I had heard about all I wanted to about Roy Rogers from my agent. He was doing quite nicely in his career. Fine, Art, but what about Dale Evans who has (a) lost her movie contract and (b) been given her walking papers by NBC radio?

When the latter took place, I immediately placed a call to Art. Sorry, his secretary informed me, he was enroute to New York to handle some business for Mr. Rogers. I did a slow burn and counted the days until the world's greatest Roy Rogers fan got back to town.

In a manner best described as less than diplomatic, I informed Mr. Rush upon his return that inasmuch as he seemed to be so busy handling the affairs of his already-successful singing cowboy and Nelson Eddy and didn't have time to properly aid me in getting my roller-coaster career straightened out, it might be best that we go our separate ways. I left him little room for argument.

Danny Winkler, a longtime friend of Joe Rivkin—in fact, he had encouraged Joe to contact me originally after having heard me on radio when I was still in Chicago—became my third agent and immediately set about to redirect my career toward the movies.

With, I was later to learn, a little help from Art Rush. While playing golf at the Lakeside Country Club one afternoon, Art had learned from Armand Schaeffer, an executive at Republic Studios, that they were planning production of a musical and were in the market for new faces. He quickly dug out the screen test I had done for Paramount and had Schaffer take a look at it.

Winkler took the ball from there and in short order I was signed to a one-year contract with Republic. Not as impressive as the seven-year deal Roy Rogers had at the time, mind you, but I was in no position to be choosy.

Two weeks later I was into rehearsal for a movie entitled *Swing Your Partner,* working with Lulu Belle and Scotty (who had made big names for themselves on the "National Barn Dance") and Vera Vague of "The Bob Hope Show." It was, in every respect, a "country musical" if ever there was one, but it *was* a musical and it *was* a movie in which I did more than walk on and off the set. Not exactly Academy Award stuff, granted, but it was a promising start.

I soon vowed never to criticize anyone who talked of how hard movie people worked. I was meeting myself coming and going. During the next year I did nine more films—including the likes of *Here Comes Elmer* and *Hoosier Holiday*—and must have toured every Army base in the southwestern United States. In my spare time I was in the recording studio.

Republic renewed my contract, a bit of good news I wanted to personally share with Mother and Dad. So while on a singing tour of Texas military bases, I stopped off in Italy for a few days. To my delight, even my parents were now showing signs of excitement about my blossoming career. And it didn't hurt my ego a bit when the studio called me during our visit, telling me to return to Hollywood immediately to begin rehearsal for yet another musical. I did an immodest shrug and told the folks good-bye, saying, "That's Hollywood."

I arrived to find that the picture had been canceled. And my confidence was not such that I wasn't quite nervous when word reached me that Herb Yates, owner of the studio, wanted to see me.

Having just returned from New York where he had attended a showing of the smash Broadway production of *Oklahoma!* he enthusiastically described the play, applauding it scene by scene. Sitting there, I allowed my fantasies to take over. Perhaps Republic Studios was thinking of doing a film version of the play and perhaps . . .

It was not a fantasy which lasted long.

"Our Roy Rogers Westerns have been doing quite well," Yates continued, "and I think they could be even better if we had a female lead who could also do some singing. I think you're what we're looking for."

His was not the most exciting proposal I had ever heard. B-Westerns were directly opposite from the way I wanted my career to go. And why me? The closest thing to a Western I had done was a small role as a saloon singer in a John Wayne shoot-em-up.

"Mr. Yates," I said, "are you sure you want me?" It was more a plea for reconsideration than a direct question.

He was sure. "Rehearsals for *The Cowboy and the Senorita* will begin next week," he said. "You're the senorita."

Period.

8

So THERE I WAS with my nose out of joint, certain my road to Broadway musical comedy had been blown up by a studio owner's brainstorm that the B-Western fans out in the hinterland wanted more song with their sagebrush. For a woman who could still remember watching large groups of down and defeated men, victims of the Depression, standing in soup lines in Chicago and sleeping beneath old newspapers on the cold cement sidewalks along Wacker Drive, I was a pretty picky lady. But not stupid.

It seemed to me the best way to get my career in Westerns over and done with was to perform so well in them that Republic would have to put me in better pictures, give me better roles.

The picture was a success, and theater managers were urging the studio to continue teaming me with Roy.

Before the year was out I had three more pictures with Roy and, when fan mail began arriving in amounts far greater than at any time in my career, it occurred to me that riding horses, holding the reins, and saying "He went thataway" wasn't the worst fate that could befall a girl.

Which isn't to say the Western movie business wasn't without its darker moments. I'm convinced to this day, in fact, that only the most ornery or lazy horses were picked for me to ride.

One afternoon as we were waiting for the shooting of a

scene, we were all sitting around listening to one of Gabby Hayes's delightfully funny stories. I was already on my horse, ready to ride whenever the director was. When Gabby delivered his punch line I broke into laughter and inadvertently dug my heels into my horse's side. I thought it was the start of the Kentucky Derby. The horse was running at a full-out gallop and I was hanging onto the saddle horn for dear life, screaming in a very unladylike manner.

Now the story begins to sound like it came directly from the pages of one of our scripts: Roy jumped on Trigger and came after me, riding up alongside and grabbing me just as I was about to tumble ankle over elbow into the hot sands of the California desert.

Then there was the time I was supposed to assert myself and punch one of the bad guys in the jaw while he was trying to carry me away in a buckboard. Still relatively unschooled in bare-knuckle brawling, I threw my supposedly fake punch just as the buckboard lurched. At the time I was wearing a ring that had three large diamonds mounted on it, one of which had belonged to my mother, another to my grandmother, and one to my aunt. It turned out there would be nothing fake whatsoever about the misguided punch. The ring, which I would never wear again while shooting, opened a gash in the man's face that you wouldn't believe. They rushed first aid to him while I rushed to my dressing room scared, sick, and more than a little embarrassed.

All in all, however, it was far more enjoyable than I had expected it would be. Roy Rogers, the object of my earlier jealousy when Art Rush was working as my agent, proved to be a delightful person. To have gained the status he was already enjoying in the business, he seemed totally unaffected. While he was prone to good-natured ribbing, constantly kidding me about my Texas twang and my problems staying atop a horse, he was always helpful, and at times demonstrated the patience of Job. He was down-to-earth, not in the least bit phony. Instead of attending one party after another to talk about his latest picture or the one he would be doing next, he was far more comfortable having a few friends over for dinner in his home.

A devoted family man, he was forever talking about his wife and two little girls, never making the point that one was adopted and the other his own. When they would come out to watch us shoot, his eyes would light up.

On the set he was easily the most popular man around among the too often unrewarded crew members who took care of such things as lighting, the cameras, and the booms. They were, in fact, all members of a bowling team which Roy sponsored, and delighted in reporting to him the results of a previous night's competition.

To this day I have never met a more giving person. When we would go on the road for personal appearances, it never ceased to amaze me how much time he spent with kids. It was no show business put-on. Just as he does today, Roy Rogers loved kids more than anything else in the world.

After it was apparent that I had been more or less permanently teamed with him, a letter arrived from home in which Mother said Dad was interested in knowing more about "this cowboy actor you're making pictures with."

To put a father's worries about his daughter to rest—after all, I was married and well past voting age—I sat down and wrote him about Roy. "He's very plain and humble," I wrote. "In fact, he reminds me a lot of [my brother] Hillman. I've not once seen him trying to upstage another actor in a scene, and no matter what comes up he seems forever to be on the side of the underdog. He does a lot of wonderful things for the people he works with. So no, you don't have to worry. He's a fine person and has become a good friend. The best way to describe Roy Rogers, I guess, is that he rings true."

And though I failed to mention it in the letter, he was a truthful person. Which was more than I could say of myself.

TOMMY WAS GRADUATING from high school, yet I had still continued with the outlandish ploy of referring to him as my little brother instead of my son. It had begun to eat at me constantly, but I had never mustered the strength to set things straight.

So there I was, graduation night, walking into the high school auditorium in virtual disguise. I wore no makeup, had arranged my hair differently, wore dark glasses, and had picked out the plainest dress I had for one of the most rewarding moments a parent can ever hope to experience.

My son would conduct the school orchestra in a piece he

had written and arranged, and then take his place with his flute as the school director took over. Tommy had become a fine musician, and I dreamed of being able to send him to music school after graduation. Even when he was just beginning to play, in fact, Caesar Petrillo, the CBS orchestra leader in Chicago, had said he had great promise and pointed out the scarcity of gifted flutists in the music world.

I was prepared to do whatever I could to spare him some of the bumpy roads I had traveled in gaining a foothold on my career. I had come to know a number of influential people in the music business, and felt sure I would be able to help with a little door-opening here and there when the time came. For the lie I had forced him to play an unwilling part in, I felt I owed him as much help as I could give him.

There were other problems. While my career seemed to be progressing nicely, little else in my life was. My marriage was on the decline. R. Dale was scoring movies for Republic and arranging for several people. His work schedule called for him to be on the job in the late afternoon and evenings, and mine was almost exactly the opposite. Neither of us considered making our careers secondary to our marriage, and it came to the unfortunate point where we really had no life together. We had allowed the Hollywood system to take hold of our lives, sending us in opposite directions.

In 1945 we were divorced.

AFTER doing nine Westerns, I had had my fill of horses and hayseed homilies, fist-fighting and shoot-outs and getting fourth billing, after Roy's horse and then Gabby Hayes. That's the way it always read: Starring Roy Rogers and Trigger, Gabby Hayes, and Dale Evans, etc., etc.

I made my march on Herb Yates's office. In my best ultimatum-delivering voice I told him that if I wasn't soon given some better roles I was prepared to quit. He carefully explained the situation to me. First, he said, you are under contract. Second, since you are, you will take the roles assigned you by the studio. Third, if you should walk out, there is a very real possibility that a suspension and legal action will be forthcoming, which could be very costly to you.

I did ten more Westerns.

But not without making an occasional wave. During a visit to Pittsburgh, I told my feelings to a reporter named Maxine Garrison. In her story for the *Pittsburgh Press* I was quoted as having said, "The heroine in a Western is always second-string. The cowboy and his horse always come first." She went on to speculate on how long I would be satisfied with being a second-stringer, pointing out my stage ambitions and desire to do musicals.

Republic wasn't the only one throwing a fit. Letters began coming in by the hundreds asking that I not quit. It was, frankly, as flattering as it was surprising. One letter came from a Roy Rogers Fan Club, with three thousand signatures affixed to it.

It was nice to know that I had a sizable audience which was evidently enjoying what I was doing, but my gut feeling was to fight it. I was becoming more and more typecast with each passing picture. I was part of Roy Rogers's movies, I was part of his road show, and soon I would be sharing the microphone with him on the Miles Laboratories-sponsored "Weekly Round-up" on NBC. I liked Roy very much personally; we had developed a close friendship and enjoyed being around each other, talking, sharing ideas. But our thoughts about our careers weren't the same. He was happy being a singing cowboy and had, in fact, done a little balking of his own when the studio suggested he play other roles. I was the one literally begging for other roles, and all I could get was another Western. And another.

In 1947 we finished making *Bells of San Angelo* at the same time my contract with Republic had run its course. I made no effort to renew it. Enough was enough. They could get themselves another cowgirl.

I WENT BACK TO RADIO, taking a job as featured singer with Jimmy Durante and Garry Moore on their network show, while waiting for the next development in my movie career to materialize. Soon Danny Winkler was calling, much to my delight, to say that RKO wanted me for the ingenue lead in a movie to be called *Show Business Out West,* starring Eddie Cantor and Joan Davis. It would be, he said, a musical comedy.

What it would actually be was a musical comedy which never got off the ground. After a long wait, I was finally informed that the project had been scrapped.

I was finally getting the idea that someone, somewhere, was trying to tell me musical comedy was not in the stars for this particular Texas dreamer.

When Republic came to the rescue, asking that I reconsider and return to the studio, I was again running pretty low on options. To my pleasant surprise it was not only prepared to offer me a better contract than the one I had allowed to lapse but, for reasons I didn't even bother trying to understand, it was prepared to allow me to work in something other than Westerns.

Acting as if I had never even left, the studio publicity department announced that "Miss Evans was slowing her pace somewhat and would soon be appearing in different roles from those she had while sharing billing with Roy Rogers."

Thus it was that, with my hair done up in the finest Lana Turner fashion and wearing long gowns rather than cowboy boots, I made my dramatic debut in a movie titled *The Trespasser* in the spring of 1947, and even got my first full-fledged screen kiss from my co-star Doug Fowley. I felt I had arrived.

In truth, that kiss was one of the strangest experiences of my life. I had watched screen heroines getting kissed thousands of times, and it looked so easy, so natural. I mean, how hard is a kiss, really?

What the moviegoer doesn't see is all the preparation that goes on beforehand. Everywhere grips and cameramen and directors are getting things prepared while you're standing there, arm in arm, in the bright lights, waiting for someone to finally say "action." You hardly know the guy you're supposed to be madly in love with, and you barely know his name. So it's a big fat nothing, no real emotion. You get it over with, hope the director doesn't call for another take, and get on with the dialogue.

Actually, the kiss came off pretty well. The movie as a whole didn't. I'll not bore you with the reviews for the simple reason that I found no reason to save any of them. I chalked it up to experience and went on a singing tour while waiting to see what was next.

I was in Atlantic City for an engagement at the Steel Pier, when one evening during my performance I looked out into the crowd and saw Art Rush and Roy (wearing a business suit, no less). It was, quite literally, like seeing friends from back home. I joined them as soon as the show ended, and learned that Roy was in New York doing a show and had talked his manager into driving down to see me. Almost a year had passed since Arlene's untimely death and Roy, for so long dispirited and lonely, seemed fine again. The kids, being looked after by a housekeeper in his absence, were also doing nicely, he said. He enthusiastically described the new house he had purchased on Lake Hughes near Lancaster, California—a ranch he called Sky Haven. The mountain home, he said, was small but comfortable, quiet, and the locale was scenic.

I told him of Tom's enlisting in the Army and, holding true to his word about not lying publicly about being my son, had listed "Dale Evans, actress" as his mother. One of the Army's public information officers had, in turn, contacted the studio's publicity department about the matter, and had been persuaded to not make the information available to any members of the press.

We had dinner together, delighted with one another's company, and eventually a number of humorous anecdotes from the filming of movies we had done together crept into the conversation. I could see it coming; cagy, Roy Rogers is not.

"Look, Dale," he said, "the movies we did together were good. An awful lot of people liked us working as a team. Why don't you come back?"

I thanked him, but no-thanked him, making it clear that it was nothing personal. He didn't press the issue further.

When my tour was completed, I returned to Hollywood to do another picture, *Slippy McGee*, which, if anything, was a bigger box office flop than had been *The Trespasser*.

Then I sought out Herb Yates and told him I was ready to return to my horse.

IT WAS GOOD to be back working with Roy and Gabby and the Sons of the Pioneers. A strong family-like atmosphere was even more evident on the set when I moved back into the fold; it was as if I had never left. Everyone seemed glad to see me, and I was aware of no sign of bitterness or resentment over my self-proclaimed absence.

Another thing which occurred to me was that Roy and I had a good rapport. We were somewhat opposites in temperament, but that seemed to provide a good balance. We were straightforward with each other (he was one of the few I had told the truth about Tommy and me, for instance) and were at ease when we had talks that would sometimes stretch on for hours.

It began to occur to me that there were far worse fates than working with Roy Rogers on a daily basis, even if he wasn't interested in musical comedy.

As if I had not missed a beat, I was back in the swing of his hectic life—doing movies, radio shows, and going on the road for personal appearances and rodeo performances. Suddenly it all began to make some sense. Maybe the old axiom about there being a place for everybody and everybody having a place had some truth to it. Before the year 1947 was completed Roy Rogers was not the only Western star listed among his field's top-ten box office moneymakers. Of course, he was number one, but Dale Evans was on the list as well.

It was late in the year, with yet another picture completed, that we left for an eight-week tour which would take us to Philadelphia, Detroit, St. Louis, and Chicago. It would be, to say the least, unforgettable. We were sitting astride our horses in the chutes of the massive Chicago Stadium, fighting off the regular preperformance butterflies while waiting for a trained animal act to be completed so we could make our galloping entrance into the spotlight.

"I just talked with the kids at home," Roy said.

"Everything okay?"

"Fine. They said to tell you hello."

It was, you'll agree, not an extraordinary conversation by any stretch of the imagination at that point. But then Roy reached into his pocket and brought out a small box. "Hold out your finger," he said.

It was a beautiful little gold ring with a ruby setting. A very thoughtful birthday gift, I immediately thought. After all, Halloween was just a few weeks away.

There was no smile on Roy's face as he asked, "What are you going to be doing New Year's Eve?"

"I don't have any plans," I answered.

"Fine," he said. "Why don't we get married then?"

His timing was perfect. Before I could even answer, the announcer was calling his name and off he rode, the "King of the Cowboys," the man I was going to say yes to just as soon as my horse could catch up to him.

9

IT PLEASES ME TO REPORT to you that, despite rumors which appeared in several of the gossip columns after it became public knowledge that Roy and I were to be married, Trigger did not serve as best man.

That particular task fell to Art Rush. Otherwise, it was far from the quiet, simple wedding both of us had planned. In an effort to sidestep a lot of Hollywood hoopla, we had accepted the invitation of Bill Likins, who owned the Flying L Ranch near Davis, Oklahoma, where we had just completed the filming of *Home in Oklahoma,* to be married there.

It was to be a simple ceremony with our parents, a few close friends, and the Likins in attendance. The Reverend Dr. Bill Alexander of nearby Oklahoma City would perform the ceremony. The roaring blizzard which invaded the state of Oklahoma just days before the wedding was not invited.

Aware of the bad weather, Roy and I left California early, taking the train instead of a plane as had been originally planned. No sooner had we arrived at the terminal in Oklahoma City than we were surrounded by a large number of newsmen who, with the help of columnist Louella Parsons, had learned our travel plans. For a half-hour we answered questions—no, the wedding would not be conducted in Old West costume; no, Trigger had not made the trip and therefore would not stand up for his owner; no, we didn't feel the millions of kids who made up the bulk of Roy's fans would consider their hero a sissy for marrying; and finally, no, we would not provide the photographers with a kiss. "We've never kissed in front of the movie cameras," Roy smiled, "so we're not going to start doing it for the papers, either."

I have to say that I would have perferred to not face a barrage of newspapermen's questions at that particular time—I was already getting quite nervous about the whole affair—but because of something which had happened a few weeks earlier, I found it difficult to be angry with Louella Parsons for having made our wedding plans public. She had done me a service for which I'll never be able to repay her.

Sitting at home one evening, just half listening to her radio show, I became more alert when I heard my name mentioned. She told of our plans to be married, did a brief rundown of some of the highlights of my career to better acquaint her listeners, I supposed, to the lady who was soon to become Mrs. Roy Rogers. And then she dropped her bombshell. "A long kept secret," she said, "is the fact that Dale Evans is the mother of a twenty-year-old son . . ."

I was stunned. I didn't know whether to scream, faint, throw a temper tantrum, or all of the above. I just sat there for a minute, convincing myself that I had actually heard correctly. And then, as it settled in, a great relief flooded over me. Now they knew; the charade was finally over. I felt a warm, welcome sense of freedom.

Soon the news had reached Tom and, worried about my reaction, he came to talk to me. I think he was surprised to find me in such high spirits. "Tom," I said, "it's the best thing that could have happened. I'm delighted; I feel like I've finally been set free. For the rest of my life I'll be grateful for what Louella Parsons did for me."

Finally the day of the wedding arrived, complete with ice, snow, and a bone-chilling wind howling outside. There is something to be said, I decided, for electing to be a June bride.

But it was cozy inside the comfortable ranch-style home of the Likins, and preparations began on schedule.

In the living room a small altar had been placed, surrounded with flowers. A male quartet was on hand, ready to begin rehearsing the numbers they would sing. And with the help of Mary Jo Rush, I set about to get ready.

By late afternoon most of the guests had arrived, telling horror stories about the weather and traveling conditions. Tom was late, having encountered car trouble, but arrived with his new fiancée Barbara Miller and her sister. All seemed in order, until someone mentioned that the pastor had still not arrived. A call to Oklahoma City brought assurance that he was on the way. After almost two hours had passed and the storm's intensity had grown worse, there was serious discussion about forming a search party to look for him. Things were getting complicated.

When Bill Alexander finally came through the front door, brushing snow from his overcoat, a loud cheer went up. And then there was laughter. Evidently one of those who believes everything he reads in the papers, he had assumed that the ceremony would be an Old West affair, and was therefore dressed in a turn-of-the-century frock-coat and a string tie.

By this time Roy had soaked his fresh white shirt in perspiration worrying about the tardiness of the minister and various other last-minute details of the wedding. Art Rush came to his rescue, finding a white shirt of his own that came close to fitting. "It was no real problem," he would say later, "I shortened the length of the sleeves with a couple of rubber bands and compensated for the fact that collar size was a bit large by tying his tie near the choking point. Agents are supposed to be able to tend to such minor problems, you realize."

The problems I was having as I completed dressing were far from minor. Sitting there, just a few minutes away from the biggest step of my life, I became panic-stricken. Doubts rolled over me; questions raced through my mind in machine-gun fashion. With divorce and unsuccessful remarriage behind me, was it right to try again? Was it right for Roy? And for his children? We had talked about all these things many times, and he had assured me that he loved me, that his children loved me and were anxious for me to become a part of their family. I knew fully well that I loved Roy and wanted to be a good mother to his children. But there was no written guarantee, no unbreakable promise that would assure success.

Horrified and uncertain, I felt alone. There was no one to whom I could go at this particular moment to talk about such doubts. I got up and walked into a dark, empty clothes closet and closed the door. And prayed harder than I had ever prayed in my life: "Dear God, you know who I am and what I am. You know the great responsibility I'm taking on by marrying this man with three motherless children. Please help me. Give me the courage and the understanding to establish a Christian home for them, a home like the one you gave me as a child."

Standing there in that dark closet, I began to feel a deep, reassuring calm come over me. I was ready to marry Roy. I quickly finished dressing and soon heard my cue. Downstairs I heard them singing "I Love You Truly."

Bill Likins met me at the foot of the stairs to escort me into the den, and we took our appointed spots near the fireplace. All was finally going according to plan. The minister was there; the guests were on hand. Mary Jo Rush, my matron of honor, was at my side. We waited for Art and Roy. And waited. For almost five minutes.

I had no idea what was taking place around the corner of the den, but if the quartet had to go through "I Love You Truly" one more time I was going to make a beeline for the door, blizzard or no blizzard.

Finally, however, they made their appearance, and the ceremony began. Roy had not even given me the traditional kiss before his best man rushed from the room, leaving a number of people with puzzled looks on their faces. "Gotta check on the fire," he said.

As he and Roy had been making their way toward the den, they had seen smoke coming from under the door to one of the bedrooms. Roy had gone in to find a wastebasket in flames and nearby curtains smoldering. While I had been waiting for him to come around the corner and marry me, he had been yanking curtains down and rushing them into the bathroom, where he threw them into the bathtub and started the water running while Art smothered the fire in the wastebasket.

And so it was, on the evening of December 31, 1947, I became Mrs. Roy Rogers with the water still running in the bathtub.

By the time the reception was over, it was necessary to call out the State Troopers to escort some of the guests to the nearby motel where they would spend the night. Nobody ever said getting married was supposed to be easy. And, after all, all's well that ends well.

The following day the storm broke. Crisp and cold, the ranch looked like a scene from a Christmas card. "It will," my new husband noted, "be a perfect night for coon huntin'!"

Thus I spent the second night of my honeymoon tramping through the cold darkness of the Flying L, listening to the baying of hounds and constantly reminding myself that Reverend Alexander had said for better *and* for worse.

THE FIRST ORDER OF BUSINESS upon our return to California was to combine our households. Roy and the children were still living on the ranch near Lake Hughes, and Tommy, now attending Southern Cal, shared my little house in North Hollywood with me. Soon we were combining a weird montage of furniture, dishes, and sundry belongings in a beautiful two-story Spanish-style home built on the side of a mountain by the late Noah Beery, Sr. It was an exciting time—opening boxes and barrels, trying to sort this and that into place. Marion Christiansen, the mother of Roy's movie stand-in Whitey, had become Roy's housekeeper, and had agreed to stay on to lend me a hand.

The thought of setting up house for a family excited me, and I was anxious to get things into place. While I was still going to appear with Roy in as many of his road-show performances as possible, the movies would have to wait. Republic, to be quite honest, didn't seem to mind, inasmuch as several of the executives were voicing worry over how their singing cowboy would do at the box office now that he was married. Having his wife on the screen with him would only serve as a constant reminder of something the studio would just as soon the fans forget. Which was fine by me. I had all I could handle and then some.

No idealist, I had anticipated some problems with Roy's children and had made every effort I could to keep them to a minimum. I saw to it that a picture of Arlene was placed in the children's rooms, and made it clear to one and all that it was not my intent to try to replace their mother. I wanted them to have wonderful memories of her, to never forget her. Occasionally we would pick flowers together and visit the cemetery, where they placed them on their mother's grave.

But as a stepmother I made little headway. Little Dusty, still too young to understand my role and having no memory of Arlene, accepted me right off the bat. The girls, on the other hand, provided a challenge. One day as I was arranging some furniture in the living room, Linda Lou came in, watched me with unsmiling eyes for a moment, and then said, "That isn't your furniture. It's my Mommy's." It angered me, but I held my tongue for a moment, and then said, "Honey, your mommy's gone to heaven, and she doesn't need this furniture anymore, so it's okay for us to use it." She said nothing, turned and walked upstairs to her room.

On another occasion I was sitting in the kitchen, having a cup of coffee and smoking a cigarette, when Cheryl came in and, without any other preface, said, "I wish you didn't smoke. My mother never smoked."

I put the cigarette out and threw the pack into the wastebasket. I quit smoking, cold turkey, that very day. No doubt it did wonders for my health, but I could not see that it had gained me much ground with the children. Nothing seemed to help. Roy, thoroughly miffed by the children's behavior, tried to help, having long talks with them but getting little positive result. "Just give them time," he would say, "and things will get straightened out. I know that they love you."

You could have fooled me.

The thought of punishing the children horrified me. I tried to reason with them instead. That was another big mistake. By trying to win friends and influence people I was doing nothing to establish my authority in the home. It finally occurred to me that I was doing us all a great disservice. Now I was not just the stepmother; I was the evil stepmother—an evil stepmother who was close to her wit's end.

Which was not the best time in the world for my agent Danny Winkler to call and advise me to find a place to sit down before he told me his news. "Dale," he said, "you are wanted for the lead in the London company of *Annie Get Your Gun.* That's the musical comedy you've been looking for so long."

No doubt Danny was all set for screams of delight and probably the sounds of immediate packing. Instead, what he heard was that the children had just been exposed to chicken pox, that we were in the midst of having an addition built onto the house, and that Tom and Barbara were just about ready to set their wedding date. "Danny," I said, "there's no way I can accept it. I couldn't possibly think of leaving right now."

"But, they want you right now."

"I'm sorry. It would have been fun."

Certainly more fun than I was having with a hostile seven-year-old and a brooding four-year-old. Daily I became more thankful that Dusty was just fifteen months old and still innocent of jealousy and resentment.

Tom, aware of the difficulties I was having, made it a point to regularly lend me moral support. He had been thrilled by my marriage and had even asked Roy one evening if he would mind his calling him Dad. I would have given anything in the world to have Cheryl or Linda Lou ask if they could call me Mom, but that day seemed to be far, far in the future.

"Have you tried taking them to Sunday school and church?" Tom asked. "Maybe God can lend a hand. Why don't you all come with me next Sunday?"

He insists to this day that he had no part in it, but I've always suspected that Tom entered into a conspiracy with Dr. Jack MacArthur on the sermon which was delivered that following Sunday: "The House That Is Built on the Rock." Any house, the message said, which was built on the rock of faith in Jesus Christ could and would be able to survive anything.

Dr. MacArthur, it seemed, was speaking directly to me. And

when his sermon was completed and the invitation extended, Tom leaned over and whispered to me: "Why don't you go? Give the Lord your life and let him help you with your struggles."

I told him that I had already made that walk, that I had been a Christian since I was ten years old. "But do you really know Christ?" he countered.

I needed time to think about it. Maybe in a couple of weeks, I said.

All the way home the sermon kept ringing in my ears. Roy was away on a hunting trip that weekend, and when we returned to the house I went immediately to my room. There, with the door closed, I got down on my knees beside the bed and cried like I had never cried before. I cried and I prayed and I cried some more. I knew suddenly what was missing in my life. Tom was right, I had not really known Jesus Christ. I had been merely using him as a touchstone, a comforting shoulder in time of need. I prayed for forgiveness and asked that the Lord allow me to live out the week. "Just let me make it until next Sunday and I will be the first person down that aisle," I asked.

The following Sunday was one of the most glorious of my life. I walked the aisle and grasped Dr. MacArthur's hand. Later I was ushered into a prayer room for consultation with a counselor. An indescribable peace flowed through my body, and I experienced a happiness I had never known before.

I was eager to share my new joy with Roy when I got home. "I've just made the greatest decision of my life," I told him. "Today I dedicated my life to Jesus Christ. It's wonderful."

He smiled and listened as I went on and on about the new feelings I was experiencing. Then, once I had quieted, he said, "I'm glad for you if it makes you happy. But be careful." With that he paused for a moment as if to emphasize his next statement. "Just don't go overboard, okay?"

I knew full well what he meant. For all his goodness, Roy was a skeptic about religion. We had discussed the subject before. He had, he said, gone to church regularly as a youngster back in Ohio, but more for the social life it afforded than the spiritual reward. Even as a boy it had puzzled him to see the same people professing their faith and being baptized over and over again as revival preachers made their annual rounds. If you do it once, he said, why is it necessary to just keep doing it over and over?

And then there was his greatest argument, one even many gifted ministers and church leaders have difficulty explaining. "I go into those hospitals and orphan homes and see those innocent little children, sick and crippled and without parents," he said, "and I have to ask myself why God would let something like that happen. It just doesn't seem right."

What he was saying when he asked me to "not go overboard," then, was to not begin a campaign to get him to walk that same aisle. Aside from extending him an invitation each Sunday to join us in going to church—which he regularly declined—I didn't pressure him. And while there were no overnight miracles in my relationship with the girls, things were getting better. We read Bible stories in the evenings, said our prayers together, and slowly but surely seemed to be getting more comfortable with each other.

Even Roy began to notice the welcome change. One evening as we were preparing for bed, he stopped at his night table, where a new Bible lay. "What's this?" he asked. In my most nonchalant manner, I glanced in his direction and said, "Oh, I got that for you since you lost your other one." Roy, who had never owned a Bible in his life, shook his head, laughed, and came to bed.

A month before Easter, Roy completed another picture, and in celebration we had a large party at our home. It was one of those evenings which, despite careful planning, had disaster written all over it from the very beginning. Roy had had a long, hard day at the studio, and I was virtually exhausted from getting things ready for the evening and making preparations for Easter.

There were many guests from show business, much "shop talk." And for me, a new and excited Christian, as the hours wore on there was a longing to share my new-found joy. Suddenly one of Roy's leading ladies confronted me with, "Evans, what has happened to you? You're not the same . . ." I started to explain that my perspective was new, different; that I had realized my responsibility in my marriage, with three stepchildren.

Apparently, Roy overheard only the last remark about "responsibility," and misunderstood. He strode over to us and bluntly told me, "If you have a problem, this is no place to talk about it," then turned on his heel and walked away. It hurt. After a few moments I excused myself, went upstairs, shed a few tears, and rejoined the party.

Later, in our bedroom, there was a strained silence between us. Roy was still standing at the window, staring into the night, when I fell asleep.

The next morning was Sunday. I was preparing to take the children to Sunday school and church when Roy came downstairs and informed me, "If you are going to church tonight, I am going with you."

That night, as we sat in the service, Roy's head was down for quite a period of time and I thought, "He's asleep, not hearing a thing . . ." At the invitation he sat bolt upright, turned to me, and declared, "Mama, I'm going down there." And go he did, accepting Jesus Christ as his Savior.

Talking of his decision later, Roy told me that as he had stood looking out the bedroom window that night, it had occurred to him that any financial provisions he might be able to leave for his children would someday be gone. The fame of being a movie star wouldn't last forever. "I just decided," he said, "that I wanted my kids to remember me for something special, something that mattered. I wanted them to remember me as a daddy who took them to church on Sundays and helped them learn how to live a good Christian life."

The next Sunday our oldest daughter, Cheryl, accepted Jesus. She and Roy were baptized Palm Sunday evening; my cup, surely, was running over! A spiritual bond was formed in our family which has never been broken.

Roy with Cheryl shortly after she came from Hope Cottage, 1941.

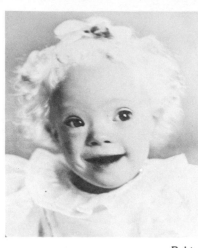

Robin

Little Robin at our home in Encino,
California.

At the Los Angeles Airport, bringing Sandy and Dodie home after adoption — Sandy from Kentucky, Dodie from Dallas, Texas (Hope Cottage).

Above: The Rogers family at Chatsworth, 1957. From left to right: Cheryl, Linda, Marion, Dusty, Sandy, Dodie, and Debbie.

Below: Dale with Debbie and Dodie at Chatsworth.

Dusty and Sandy at the ranch near Chatsworth, 1957.

A Thanksgiving prayer — November 1962.
Seated (clockwise) are Dusty, 16; Dodie, 10;
Dale; Debbie, 10; and Sandy, 15.

Ready to eat — Thanksgiving, 1962.

Sandy in his Army
uniform — 1965.

Top: Playing poker with Trigger in *Son of Paleface* (1954) with Bob Hope and Jane Russell. *Left:* Still from the Roy Rogers and Dale Evans T.V. show. *Above:* Roy and Dale with Pat Brady and Bullet in a still from the T.V. show.

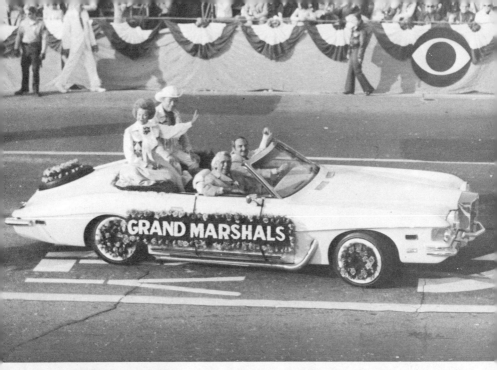

Top: The Tournament of Roses Parade — New Year's Day, 1977. Roy and Dale were first husband-and-wife team in the history of the event to serve as Grand Marshals. Art Rush is riding up front with the driver.
Left: Dale with son Tom Fox, Minister of Music at Arcade Baptist Church in Carmichael, California, at the Festival of Faith in Jerusalem, February 1978.
Above: Roy and Pat Brady on a hunting trip during the 1950s. *Next page:* Happy Trails to you! — a rodeo appearance.

Part Three

Partners

*A*n estimated two million people had jammed the sidewalks and parkway along Colorado Boulevard from Orange Grove Avenue to Sierra Madre, a five-mile ribbon of asphalt familiar to television viewers throughout the Free World. It was the morning of New Year's Day, 1977, and the traditional Tournament of Roses Parade had again turned Pasadena into a wild celebration of sight and sound.

The morning air carried the scent of a newborn day, a crisp, clean smell that brought a pleasant and welcome relief from the eye-stinging pollution which so frequently spills across the Los Angeles basin and backs up against the San Gabriel Mountains.

Earlier, while the city was still masked by darkness, thousands of cars arriving from a maze of directions had spilled from the bumper-to-bumper freeways onto the exit ramps, and their occupants had hurried to find their way to favored viewpoints along the parade route. For some the wait would stretch for hours, but it was time deemed well spent. A good vantage point from which to watch the pageantry of the Tournament of Roses, the parade to end all parades, is as coveted as a fifty-yard-line ticket to the Rose Bowl game held later in the festive day.

Now, with the waiting over, a restless stir of anticipation rumbled through the crowd. Those on hand to serve us eyewitnesses, as well as the two hundred fifty million who would watch from the comfort of their living rooms, readied for their initial glimpse of the first husband-and-wife team in the colorful affair's eighty-seven-year history to share the honor of being

Grand Marshals. The honor had been dealt to Roy Rogers and Dale Evans, motion picture and singing stars whose closely-woven careers had spanned three generations.

There, amidst the marching bands, the prize-winning flower-draped floats, the gaily costumed riders and baton-twirling majorettes, the King of the Cowboys and the Queen of the West were clearly the centerpieces of the celebration.

They represented much to many. To some they were still Saturday afternoon heroes, a welcome reminder of younger days when there were, indeed, still heroes. To others, they were living monuments to the good which is still so much a part of the American Way—two proud, strong people afraid neither of waving the flag nor publicly admitting their faith in God.

It was appropriate, then, that the theme of the day was "The Good Life." For Roy and Dale, who just the evening before had quietly celebrated their twenty-ninth wedding anniversary, the theme fit comfortably.

As the white open convertible, with the honored couple seated in the back and their longtime friend and manager Art Rush riding up front, moved into the complex pattern of the parade, cheers began to echo through the morning air. And, almost as if it had been rehearsed, a massive amateur chorus of onlookers broke into a song which had been written by Dale Evans and sung so often by both of them that it had become something of an anthem for the Western movie world: "Happy trails to you . . ."

There was an electricity about the mood of the crowd, something which went beyond the festive atmosphere generally reserved for such events. It was as if those who lined the route, standing twenty deep in many places, were reaching out to the two familiar symbols of the parade's theme—a man and a woman who, despite their successes and good fortune, had remained untarnished by the ambition and greed which had turned the first half of the 1970s into a national nightmare of deceit, deception, and disillusionment.

It was a time of intense emotion, not only for those standing along the route or seated in the jam-packed bleachers, but for Roy Rogers and Dale Evans as well.

"I had ridden Trigger along that same route a number of times," Roy would later recall, "but it was never anything like this. Dale and I had enjoyed riding on various floats in years past, but this was different. The crowd reached out to us with an almost overwhelming spirit of warmth and acceptance that I had never felt before. It was one of the most wonderful experiences I've ever had."

"There are times when we're all guilty of taking things for granted," said Dale. "But this day was something special. When you stop and think about it, it is an enormous responsibility to have been chosen to exemplify the 'Good Life' in the parade. Serving as Grand Marshals has to be one of the most rewarding things that has ever happened to us."

10

THE YEARS IMMEDIATELY FOLLOWING *Dale's and Roy's marriage was a time of great prosperity for the King of the Cowboys. He seemed to have a death lock on the position of number-one Western box office draw, a state of affairs which, with a little urging from Art Rush, prompted Republic to sign him to a second seven-year contract at a one-hundred percent salary increase. A seventeen-day rodeo appearance in Chicago netted him a staggering three hundred thousand dollars, and hundreds of theaters across the country were waiting in line for him to appear on their stages. With Art Rush, who had also returned to managing Dale's affairs, taking full advantage of a clause in Roy's contract which gave him all rights to his name, voice, and likeness for commercial tie-ups, Roy Rogers merchandise was hard to avoid. In addition to such items as charm bracelets, neckerchiefs, toy guns, lariats, clothing, and games, millions of comic books were being sold: four Roy Rogers novels were being published annually; Roy Rogers songbooks were hot items. And there was the newly-opened Roy Rogers Dude Ranch near Las Vegas.*

Over two thousand fan clubs were in operation in the United States, and a chapter in London reported fifty thousand fans— the largest individual fan club in the world. Anxious to make the clubs meaningful, Roy had his staff organize meetings to be held in theaters, and requested that Bill Alexander, the minister who had married him and Dale, write a "Cowboy's Prayer" which could be used to open the meetings of the Roy Rogers Rider's Club, which grew to over five million members. From his organizational efforts sprang a nationwide Roy Rogers Safety Awards program, which stressed caution to elementary-school students the nation over.

Walt Disney Studios borrowed Roy and the Sons of the Pioneers to star in a movie entitled Melody Time, *and something of a Hollywood landmark was reached when Roy Rogers and Trigger were asked to put their hand and hoof prints in the cement courtyard of the famed Grauman's Chinese Theater. The results of a survey made by* Life *magazine, asking children what person they would most like to resemble, were split among Franklin Roosevelt, Abraham Lincoln, and Roy Rogers.*

Soon he and Dale would begin appearing on a weekly "Roy Rogers Show," sponsored by Quaker Oats for the Mutual radio network. And though Dale Evans would be replaced by such names as Jane Frazee, Francis Ford, and Adele Mara in her husband's movies in 1948, she remained a familiar and popular part of his personal appearance act, riding her horse Pal, a Trigger look-alike purchased for her by Roy.

THINGS WERE MOVING so fast that I was having a hard time keeping up with them. It was, to say the least, an exciting time. Soon I was back making movies with Roy, the studio having evidently decided that no box office disasters would occur if husband and wife were teamed together. We were doing recordings together for RCA Victor, some of them my own compositions like "May the Good Lord Take a Likin' to You," "Hazy Mountain," and "Aha, San Antone," which sold over two hundred thousand copies. We had the radio show to do, personal appearances to make, and occasionally a much-needed rest stop.

The latter, it seemed, was always of short duration. Still, our home life prospered. Our family drew closer together, and, in a sense, expanded when, much to my delight, Tom and Barbara were married.

Then, shortly after our second anniversary, I heard some news I had never expected to hear again. During a physical examination I took just before Roy and I were married, the doctor had told me that there was no chance of my having any more children without undergoing extensive surgery. But in December of 1949, my gynecologist told me, "I don't care what you've been told. Unless I've somehow forgotten what I've learned about my business, you are approximately six weeks pregnant." Roy and I were both delighted.

It was not an easy pregnancy. In my second month I came down with a case of German measles. Twice the doctor ordered me to bed to prevent the possibility of miscarriage. A blood count taken in my seventh month showed that I was Rh negative and Roy was positive, a situation which could present some problems for the baby but which the doctors felt they could take care of.

Every new problem only made me more aware of how badly I wanted this baby. The difficulties and the discomfort would be a small price to pay for the baby I dearly hoped would be a girl.

My wish came true on August 26, 1950, when seven-and-one-half-pound Robin Elizabeth Rogers came into the world in the delivery room of Hollywood Presbyterian Hospital.

After spending most of the night pacing the floor, Roy rode as the Grand Marshal of the Sheriff's Rodeo the following day, and immodestly informed ninety thousand people that he was the proud father of a new baby girl. Returning to the hospital that evening, he stopped by the nursery window before coming to my room.

"Honey," he said, "she's beautiful; she's got little ears just like yours."

It was hard to imagine being any happier. We couldn't know how quickly our world could turn upside down.

Roy Rogers, his face paled and his eyes mirroring pain, replaced the receiver and looked in the direction of Art Rush. For a moment there was a discomforting silence. Then Roy said, "She knows."

Only an hour earlier, filled with the excitement and relief that generally accompanies the doctor's announcement that mother and child can be dismissed, he had been making preparations to go to the hospital and pick up his wife and new daughter, Robin. But before he left, a call had come from Art, advising him that it was urgent that they talked before he went to the hospital.

Carrying out the most difficult task his position as manager and close friend had ever demanded, Art Rush had brought tragic news. For several days a team of specialists had conducted endless tests on the new Rogers child, and had concluded that she was suffering from Mongolism, a congenital condition which involves mental retardation and physical malformation. There was also evidence of a heart condition. Once certain of their diagnosis, the doctors had informed Art, seeking his advice on how the parents should be told.

"It seemed too cruelly wrong," Art says, "for something like that to be happening to two people like Roy and Dale, people who had worked so hard to help afflicted youngsters in hospitals and orphanages, people who had put their faith in God and lived Christian lives. When I heard the news it was, without question, the lowest and most desperate moment of my life. But someone had to tell Roy."

Together they would determine how best to break the news to Dale. She had, immediately after Robin's birth, been assured that all was well. When, in days past, she had voiced mild concern over the fact that she had been allowed only short visits with her baby while other mothers were allowed far more time, she had simply been told that little Robin needed her rest. But up until the day she was to be released from the hospital, Dale had been given no real reason to expect the crushing news that was to come.

Even as Roy and Art talked she was enthusiastically preparing to leave, when one of the nurses stopped by. "Are they going to let you take the baby home with you?" she innocently asked. Dale's heart began to pound.

"Is there any reason why I shouldn't?"

A look of horror immediately spread across the nurse's face. Dale's response was proof enough that she had no indication her child was not completely healthy and normal. The visiting nurse broke into tears. "Mrs. Rogers," she said, "I'm so sorry. I thought you knew . . . "

"Knew what?"

"You had best let your doctor tell you," the nurse said. "I'm so very sorry. I've made a terrible mistake." And with that she ran from the room.

Dale, terrified, reached for the nearby telephone and called her husband. Yes, Roy gently told her, something was wrong. He had just found out about it himself and was on his way to the hospital.

I HAVE NEVER SEEN the kind of inner strength shown by Dale once the shock of the doctor's news had passed. Oh, she cried—we both did—and spent a lot of sleepless nights at first, but as soon as she had been told of the situation she just rolled up her sleeves and went to work to do whatever was necessary.

The doctors explained Robin's condition to us in a very straightforward manner, making it clear that they had reached their combined decision only after doing all the tests they had available to them. They told us that she had not responded well in the tests. Her muscle tone was poor; she was listless most of the time and had great difficulty eating. All of the physical characteristics of a Mongoloid child were there.

Aware that their judgment was painful, they went on to explain that the lifespan of children with such a condition was often short and suggested it might be better for everyone concerned if Robin was placed in a hospital where she could receive professional care. They knew, they said, that to suggest parents give up a newborn child sounded cruel, but to do so might save even greater sorrow in time to come. The most discouraging news was that medical science had found no cure for Mongolism.

We were both heartsick at the news, angry at the medical profession for not having found a way to make our baby healthy, and frustrated by the decision the doctors had told us we were facing. Suddenly the world seemed to have turned upside down. One minute we were anxiously anticipating taking our new baby home and the next, men of great knowledge in such matters were advising us to send her away.

Dale was crying as I had never seen her cry. I knelt down beside here bed. "Honey," I said, "God sent little Robin to us and he'll help us take care of her. We're all going home."

It was a decision reached without benefit of medical knowledge or, really, even a good idea of what to expect, but it was one we've never regretted. In fact, it still frightens me to think of what an empty spot in our lives there would have been if we had followed the recommendation given us that evening in the hospital.

Which isn't to say we were able to resign ourselves to the doctors' diagnosis. We constantly looked for signs—any signs—which might prove them wrong. Maybe the narrow, slanted eyes were a common characteristic of Mongolism, but I had narrow, slanted eyes myself, and so did my sisters. We sought out other specialists, praying to find one who would tell us all the others were mistaken. We did a great deal of whistling in the dark.

It took a conversation with the head pediatrician at the Mayo Clinic to convince us to stop chasing rainbows and get on with the business of living life the way it was and the way it would be. I had taken a number of photographs of Robin with me for him to look at, hoping he might detect something which would prompt him to suggest we bring her in to see him. He looked at the pictures for only a few seconds. "It would be," he said, "a waste of your time to bring her here. And very demanding on the child. There's nothing I can do to help you."

I thanked him and was preparing to leave when he stopped me. "Mr. Rogers," he said, "if I might, I'd like to suggest something. Just go home and love her. She's a special little girl, you know, and she needs your love. I know. I've got one just like her at home."

Love was something Robin was getting in large helpings. Dale watched over her constantly, doing everything within her power to see that the new baby was well taken care of. Despite the fact that we had, on the advice of the doctor, hired a full-time nurse for Robin, it was Dale who was there to walk with her when she cried in the night. It was Dale who encouraged Robin to grip a small sterilized perfume bottle filled with milk and fitted with a miniature nipple. Day or night, even the slightest whimper from Robin had her mother at her side.

The concern of others was also very apparent. The press had been told only that Robin had been born with a congenital heart ailment, and letters of concern poured in from people promising prayers and offering words of support.

And the other children immediately took their fragile little sister to their hearts, constantly watching over her, ever ready to help with her baths or feedings. It gave me great joy to see how their attitude toward Dale had also changed.

They had no doubt sensed the hurt in Dale when she returned home, and each in his and her own way tried to do what he or she could to lift her spirits. Cheryl picked some wild flowers and placed them on Dale's bed with a note attached saying, "I love you," and Dusty colored a large picture of Pal, Dale's horse, and left it on her dressing table inscribed, "To my Mother." Linda outlined her hand on a piece of cardboard and sprayed it silver as her love offering.

If there was any doubt remaining in Dale's mind about her being fully accepted by the children, it disappeared on Mother's Day. Cheryl presented her with a card bearing the following message:

> Thanks a lot for all the things that you've done for me. You've straightened me out on a lot of things I was alone in. And when I needed comforting and experienced advice, you were always there to tell me what I wanted to know. You came to live with us at rather a bad time, with Daddy so sad, and two little girls who were naughty, and a little boy who needed a mother's love that he had never known, and that the youngest of those girls had had for only three years. The older girl, when she was smaller, always kept her sorrows and problems in her, and even when you had problems of your own you were always there by our sides and you helped make our Daddy a Christian. I can't find anything fancy to say, but thanks from all of us and we really, really love you.

To this day Dale still has that card. I'm pleased that she has. Almost as pleased as I am that my daughter wrote it.

WHEN OUR BUSINESS MANAGER and Art suggested a six-weeks road tour, which they felt should include Dale, she initially refused, pointing out the need for her to remain home with Robin. It was a tour unlike any we had done in years, and her initial suspicions were that it had been designed just to get her away from the daily pressures of tending the baby.

"A Western variety show booked into smaller cities in the middle of the winter," she said, standing her ground, "doesn't even make sense."

It was Jim Osborne, a business manager who believes in stating the facts, who persuaded her just as he had earlier persuaded me. For several weeks a potential problem had been brewing with Republic Studios, and there was a very real danger the problem could develop into one which could be financially disastrous. Republic had announced plans to sell a series of my earlier movies to television—a direct violation of my contract—and the entire matter was up in the air. Osborne, who looked after the running of Roy Rogers Enterprises, admitted fear that allowing Republic to go through with such a deal could prove disastrous for us.

So Jim talked plain dollars and cents to Dale. While he knew she had plenty to worry about, he said, it was a hard cold fact that things could get bad if Republic was allowed to carry out its plan. And since the expenses of a full-time nurse and medical attention for Robin were claiming a large amount of our earnings, the tour, which would gross something in the neighborhood of two hundred eighty thousand dollars, was necessary.

Thus, once convinced by the doctors that it would be a good idea for Robin to stay with our nurse at her home in the valley where it was warmer and drier, Dale agreed. We finished taping several of our radio shows, rehearsed some new songs, and were soon on our way, with a touring company of thirty-five, for a bus caravan through the Midwest.

Our last stop before leaving town was at the doctor's office, where Dale was again assured that Robin, despite the fact her heart condition had been diagnosed as serious, would be in no danger while we were gone.

Back in the car, Dale let her reservations about the trip surface for the first time in weeks. "If only," she said, "someone would give us some hope." I reached over to the glove compartment, pulled out a small Bible, and handed it to her. She smiled, gave me a quick kiss, and nodded. We were on our way.

Aside from an accident near Hamburg, Iowa, in which the

horse van I had designed for Trigger went through a lot of crazy motions, the trip went fine. My trainer Glenn Randall was making his way to Saint Jo, where we were scheduled to perform, when the trailer threw a wheel. The animals were quite shaken up; Trigger wasn't injured, but Bullet, a trained German shepherd we had been using in our last few movies, suffered a broken tail and spent what was to be his first live performance in the vet's office.

By the time we returned to California, we had appeared in twenty-six cities and traveled twenty thousand miles. And during the hectic six weeks, never a night went by that we didn't make two long distance phone calls—one to the kids at home, the other to Robin's nurse.

Robin was never out of our minds, but the trip did Dale a world of good. With things like rehearsals, travel arrangements, and the myriad other responsibilities that go with keeping a road show on the road, she stayed busy. The tension which had been with her constantly since returning from the hospital began to disappear.

And while we both missed our own kids, we made it a point to visit as many youngsters in hospitals along the way as possible. Believe me, you'll never find a more appreciative audience than a children's ward, or play to a group that tugs at your heart so strongly. For instance, at St. Luke's Hospital in Aberdeen, South Dakota, after our last song and handshake, the entire polio ward broke into tears when we announced that we had to be going. Walking out that door, you can rest assured, was no easy chore.

By the time we got back home, both of us had matured in our thinking about how best to care for Robin. When the nurse who had been working for us became ill and no longer able to work, we soon hired a lady who insisted that it would be best for her to keep Robin in her home at least for a while. Her reasons were valid and in the best interest of our daughter, but I doubt that we would have even considered it earlier, no matter how convincing she was.

But we had already discussed finding a place in the valley where the climate was warmer and the air dryer, something Robin dearly needed. So we agreed to let the nurse take her into her home until we made the move. Dale saw to it that that time wasn't long in coming.

Soon we moved into a Spanish-style ranch house in the San Fernando Valley. It was as close to perfection as we could make it. There was room for everyone, a swimming pool, a vegetable garden, a fruit orchard and a comfortable place for the dogs. The most special aspect of the newly named five-acre Double R Bar Ranch, however, was a small private apartment built especially by my dad and uncle for Robin. There, where she would live with her nurse, she could enjoy the quiet and privacy which the doctors said was necessary because of her tendency to become nervous at the slightest disturbance.

When she was ten months old she moved into her new quarters. The Rogers family, much to the delight of everyone, were all back under the same roof. The move seemed to do Robin a world of good. Her muscle control had shown improvement, and it was possible to put her in a stroller and make a tour of the ranch occasionally, letting her watch the dogs and the ducks and the chickens and the other children. She would sit with Dale at the piano, enjoying the soft music her mother would play. The sight of Dusty or Cheryl or Linda was all that was necessary to bring a sparkle to her little blue eyes.

For all her problems, her frailty, her handicaps, she was a happy, loving little girl who spread a warmth throughout our family I will not even attempt to describe. Suffice it to say Robin Elizabeth Rogers was someone special, and everyone in our home knew it. She was, as Dale had often said, more like an angel than a human being. The description was as accurate as it was beautiful.

She brought a rare kind of peace to our home. I can remember so many evenings that I would get home from the studio, tired and not in the best mood in the world, and would go straight out to see her. There in her little house, as I talked with her and played with her, everything would suddenly be okay. More than once Dale mentioned having the same feeling after spending time with Robin.

There was one thing the doctors missed on. They had told us that if a child does not smile by the time it is three months old, there is a strong likelihood that, because of the mental retardation, it never will. But Robin had a beautiful smile, and used it often.

Shortly after our move Dale received a call from Father Harley Wright Smith of the St. Nicholas Episcopal Church in Encino, inviting us to attend Sunday services. "I'm interested in you," he said, "and that baby. I want you to know that I feel you did the right thing by bringing her home with you. God has a real purpose for that child, and I'm certain you will learn wonderful lessons from her."

We were soon regular visitors to Father Smith's church and, when Robin was sixteen months old, she was dedicated and baptized there. At the same time Dale, Cheryl, Linda, and I were confirmed and joined the church.

11

IN THE SPRING OF 1951 the fuse which had been smoldering on the Roy Rogers–Republic Studios powder keg began burning hurriedly toward an explosion. His contract had expired on May twenthy-seventh and he refused to sign a new one unless Republic granted him the right to do television. This relatively new entertainment field had not only gained an immediate foothold on the nation, but was turning a number of former motion picture actors into wealthy men. William Boyd had had the foresight to purchase all of his "Hopalong Cassidy" pictures, and had in turn sold them to television. Almost overnight his career rose from the ashes to an even higher level of stardom that he had enjoyed in theaters during his heyday in Hollywood.

Republic, acutely aware of the financial windfall Boyd had come into, quietly went about editing fifty-seven of Roy's pictures down to fifty-three minutes of running time to fit television's format, and Herb Yates sent a telegram to the leading advertising agencies in the country to advise them of their availability. As soon as Roy and Art Rush became aware of the studio's plan, they went to their attorney Fred Sturdy and asked that he get an injunction against Yates and Republic immediately. A unique clause in Roy's contract, stating that he retained the rights to his name, voice, and likeness for any and all commercial ventures, blocked the studio's attempt to sell his pictures to television.

But one problem led to another. Quaker Oats, evidently concerned that the Rogers movies would eventually turn up on television under the sponsorship of someone other than themselves, did not renew the contract for the weekly Roy Rogers radio show.

Suddenly, after twelve years as the motion picture industry's top-drawing Western star, Roy Rogers had no movie contract, no radio contract, and no television contract. And, as he and his business associates well knew, the roaring success of Roy Rogers Enterprises would continue only for as long as the King of the Cowboys was a familiar face and voice to the nation.

The pace of his business life, then, would suddenly pick up to a pace he had never experienced, even when he was starring for Republic by day and making personal appearances by night. There was preparation of his suit against the studio to get underway, and Art left immediately for New York to discuss the possibility of a television contract with network executives and potential sponsors. And Paramount Studios, taking advantage of Roy's sudden independent status, had signed him to make a picture with Bob Hope and Jane Russell, to be entitled Son of Paleface.

In ever-cautious Madison Avenue offices, Art soon became aware that securing a commitment for a TV show was not going to be an easy task. The concern voiced by those with whom he spoke was the outcome of the suit Roy had filed. If he failed to win and Republic was successful in getting his old pictures on television, it would hardly make good business sense to have him doing thirty-minute made-for-TV shows. The direct competition with hour-long shows, which were already filmed, edited, and just waiting for commercial spots to be dropped into the appropriate places, would just be too great.

While Rush was knocking on doors in New York, Roy was busy back in Hollywood. He had the Paramount picture to do and, perhaps more importantly, an idea first proposed by Al Rackin, Roy's and Dale's publicity director, to carry out. Rackin had suggested the formation of their own motion picture company to produce a thirty-minute movie, to be titled Presenting Roy Rogers, King of the Cowboys, *which could be taken directly to potential sponsors.*

With Son of Paleface *scheduled to begin production shortly, time became a major adversary to the Roy Rogers cause. Roy, Dale, Pat Brady, and a small but dedicated crew set to work and, with an around-the-clock effort, put together an action-packed film in five days. A print was hurriedly shipped to Rush.*

By this time, wearied and disappointed by three weeks of negative responses, Art had decided to return to Los Angeles to rest and construct a new plan of attack. Sitting on the train, he tried to plan his client's next move, but the trying experiences in New York had so drained him that all he could think of was the bad news he was carrying home with him. He had pursued every avenue he was aware of, even going so far as to make return trips to several advertising agencies who had already given him earlier nos. The possibility of Roy's films being sold to television by Republic had defeated him at every turn.

"Out of sheer desperation," Rush remembers, "I went back to the offices of the Benton and Bowles ad agency and talked with Walter Craig, their vice-president. I knew General Foods was one of their clients, and spent an hour trying to convince him that a tie-up between his client and mine would be beneficial to all concerned. Walter said he would do some checking and let me know.

"He didn't say no, but there was little reason to get excited about his 'doing a little checking.' What it all boiled down to was that I was returning to Los Angeles empty-handed."

The train was nearing Chicago when a porter rang the buzzer of Art Rush's compartment, awakening him to deliver a telegram. From Walter Craig, it read, Great seeing you. Have talked with sponsors. Very interested. You must go to Battle Creek on July 11 for presentation for radio and TV. Believe deal will jell.

Art read the wire several times, and then noticed that an open Bible he had been reading when he fell asleep was still on his lap. His eyes fell on Matthew 6:8: " . . . your Father knoweth what things ye have need of, before ye ask him."

ON JULY EIGHTH Art was back on the train, headed for Battle Creek, Michigan, armed with the film, a projector, a screen, and several large boxes of display material with which he hoped to convince Post Cereals, one of the divisions of General Foods, to sponsor "The Roy Rogers Show" on TV and radio.

Two days later, a gathering of General Foods officials were telling him they were prepared to sign a contract to sponsor a Roy Rogers series. It was, in a sense, one of those good news-bad news situations. The good news, of course, was that Post Cereals was eager to associate with Roy Rogers. The bad news was that the contract would include an escape clause, which would protect the potential sponsor in the event Roy lost his court battle with Republic.

Everything hinged on the outcome of the trial.

INSTEAD OF SITTING around, worrying, and waiting for the trial date to arrive, we decided to get busy with the production of the TV series, so we could be ready to go on the air if and when the judge said the magic word.

For all the time I had spent around movie lots, I really knew very little about the organization and workings of a production company. But we managed to put one together—writers, cameramen, a crew, and a cast—and got to work. We were, at best, flying by the seat of our pants, but we were flying fast. I've never seen a group of people work so hard for such long hours.

We had decided that the format of the TV show would closely follow the kinds of story lines we had used in the movies. Each episode would be a new story, with only the setting and characters the same. Mineral City, located in Paradise Valley, would be our mythical TV home. I would play the prosperous owner of the Double R Bar Ranch, and Dale would be the proprietor of the local Eureka Cafe. As in our movies, there would be no real romance—just friendship and a combining of efforts to solve the problems and right the wrongs the scriptwriters came up with.

The permanent members of the cast would include Dale, Trigger, Bullet, and Pat Brady, who had moved in to play my movie sidekick in several pictures after Gabby had left. I was tickled to death when he agreed to become one of our regulars. His mode of transportation, an old army jeep we had tricked up to do all manner of crazy things and called Nellybelle, would get almost as many laughs as Pat in the years to come.

Dale's horse Pal created something of a problem. Using two palominos in rodeo performances had worked nicely, but on film it became a little confusing since Pal and Trigger looked so much alike. So I bought her a buckskin gelding with a beautiful black mane and tail whom she named Buttermilk.

We shot our exteriors on the old Iveson Ranch, where Westerns had been shot since the days of silent pictures, and used an old Western street on the Goldwyn Studios lot for Mineral City.

We had already finished four films when it finally came time to go to court. I seriously doubt that U. S. Judge Pierson M. Hall has ever had a more unusual-looking witness in his courtroom than I was when the trial begain on October 18, 1951. I was already involved in the shooting of *Son of Paleface,* and therefore spent my time running back and forth between the courtroom and location. On several occasions during the four and one-half weeks of hearings there on the second floor of the Los Angeles Federal Building, I took the stand in full makeup and wearing some of the gaudiest outfits I've ever worn in my life.

Judge Hall, however, wasn't one to make judgment on looks, choosing instead to deal with the facts of the case he was presiding over. He eventually handed down a ruling that granted a permanent injunction restraining Republic from selling the films to television.

I need not tell you that there was considerable celebrating in the Roy Rogers camp upon hearing the decision. Even the fact that Meyer Lavenstein, the general counsel for Republic, immediately stated that he would appeal the ruling did little to dampen our spirits.

We were back in business. Soon it was announced that in December "The Roy Rogers Show" would go on television and radio under a dual contract agreement between NBC and Post Cereals.

DALE WAS MEETING HERSELF coming and going and, to my amazement, seldom showed signs of tiring. How she managed to get done the things she did in the span of a single day, I'll never know. I'll never forget one day, early in our marriage, when the publicity department sent a photographer out to the house. They had asked that we dress in full Western outfits. When I finished dressing, I went into Dale's dressing room and found her, outfitted in boots, hat, Western skirt, and blouse, sitting at the sewing machine working on Easter dresses for the girls. I've thought at times that if she could figure some way to avoid sleeping she would be the happiest person in the world.

One afternoon she returned home before I did to find the doctor there—Robin had suffered a severe series of convulsions. For the next week her condition remained serious. Then finally she began to show signs of improvement.

The convulsions, however, had left her very weak; so weak, in fact, that she was no longer able to stand in our laps as she so loved to do, or to sit in her stroller outside and watch the other children play. The doctor recommended more physical therapy sessions, and said it would be necessary to fit her for braces between her feet to prevent her throwing a hip out of joint when she tried to stand. Dale managed to attend each therapy session with Robin and her special nurse, while never missing a beat in her professional life.

She had become an inspiration to us all without even knowing it. All I had to do when I felt myself falling into a state of feeling tired or discouraged by all that needed to be done was to look to her energy and enthusiasm and draw strength from her. It was Dale as much as the efforts of the doctors and physical therapists who had Robin's strength back to near normal by the time her second Christmas rolled around.

There was a warmth and sharing in that holiday season that I could never remember having experienced before. With the tribulations of uncertainty and court suits finally past, and Robin's strength returning, and relatives coming to make it a real old-fashioned family reunion, everyone was in high spirits.

We had long discussions about what Robin's present should be. Finally, we settled on Dusty's suggestion that she be given a toy piano which she could play with in her crib. Cheryl asked for the responsibility of writing Robin's letter to Santa.

On Christmas Eve, Dale and I went to church and said a prayer of thanks for Robin—a thanks for the joy and love she had brought to our household. We both knew that she would have all too few Christmases with us, that maybe even this one would be the last, but we had decided not to dwell on the future, to instead enjoy the time given us.

As THE NEW YEAR got underway, it became immediately obvious that the pace would not slow. Art had booked us to do eighteen performances in twelve days at the Houston Fat Stock Show in late January. Dale, always hesitant to leave Robin, agreed more readily this time, since the trip to Texas would afford her an opportunity to stop by Italy and pay a visit to her parents.

And it would give me a chance to meet a man named J. B. Ferguson. Before we left California I had received a telegram from him, offering me two hundred thousand dollars for Trigger. A wealthy Texas oilman who already owned an impressive stable of thoroughbreds and quarter horses, he had indicated in his telegram that he wished to buy Trigger as a birthday gift for his young son. Frankly, I didn't even think about it again after reading the message, and as we were busy preparing to leave I didn't even get around to answering it. In years past I had received numerous offers to buy Trigger and never considered any of them. And, it seemed to me, any offer of that kind of money had to come from someone with a rather broad sense of humor.

I found out upon our arrival in Texas that it was no joke. Hundreds of children, brought to the train station by their parents, were waiting, all voicing concern over the possibility that I was going to sell my horse. The whole crazy thing had blown completely out of proportion before I even knew what it was all about.

A story in the Houston paper had told of the offer, quoted Mr. Ferguson to the effect that he was deadly serious, and gave the impression that I was seriously considering the offer. Trigger was almost nineteen, the reporter pointed out, and now I had Trigger, Jr., a beautiful seven-year-old Tennessee Walker which we had used in several of our movies, so the sale of Trigger would hardly leave me without a horse.

I made it as clear as I knew that Trigger was not for sale at any price, but that didn't calm the storm. When we reached our hotel, there were stacks of telegrams and telephone messages urging me not to go through with the sale. Back in California, letters would soon arrive from kids throughout the country, filled with pennies and nickels and dimes. The gist was, if ol' Roy was in such a financial bind that it looked necessary to sell his horse, maybe the contents of piggy banks from sea to shining sea could provide the needed financial help.

Hoping to set the issued to rest, I met with J. B. Ferguson in a giant press conference at my Shamrock Hotel suite, thanked him for his generous offer and told him I would not sell Trigger for all the money in Texas. The crisis passed, and back in Los Angeles secretaries shook their heads at the task of returning money to loyal Trigger fans.

AT THEIR HIGHLY SUCCESSFUL 1952 PERFORMANCES in Houston, the concern Roy and Dale have for children, as well as their commitment to their faith, was strongly in evidence. As stated in the contract they had signed with the promoters of the affair, four thousand underprivileged and handicapped children were in the audience for the opening performance.

When trainer Glenn Randall asked Roy what had prompted him to begin stationing Trigger and his trailer outside the show-grounds for two hours prior to each show so that youngsters

could see the horse and ask Randall questions, Roy's explanation was simple: "If those kids had the money, they would be
inside where they could see the show."

The stock show officials had agreed to allow the show to
be televised and later shown on a General Foods-sponsored
show for the benefit of shut-ins and children who had been
unable to attend.

And for the first time, Roy Rogers strayed from the traditional
Western music his fans had become so familiar with, closing
each performance with an inspirational God-and-country finale.

Then, there was the matter of a letter he had recently received
from a young fan, saying that he liked to go to church but
that some of his friends had tried to convince him it was a
"sissy" thing to do. He asked Roy's opinion. "Dale," Roy said,
"I'm not much of a speaker, but I'm thinking seriously about
answering that youngster's question publicly. What do you
think?"

"I think," she said, "it would be wonderful." The following
Sunday, at a matinee performance, he did so, and prompted
the following report by Houston Chronicle writer Charlie Evans:

> One of the best sermons we have ever heard was delivered
> Sunday. And it wasn't from the pulpit of a church. It was from
> the center of the Coliseum rodeo arena, delivered by cowboy star
> Roy Rogers.
>
> At the Sunday matinee Rogers asked how many of the young-
> sters in the stands had been to Sunday school or church that
> morning. Then he advised, "All you little cowboys and cowgirls
> out there, be sure to go to Sunday school. You might hear some
> of your little friends say it's sissy to go to Sunday school. But
> don't you believe 'em. Going to Sunday school is the best way
> in the world to get started right in life," Roy told the youngsters.
>
> When he had finished, we heard a couple of youngsters sitting
> next to us talking. Said one: "You see, we better start going to
> Sunday school again. Roy Rogers said for us to."
>
> And we imagine many others thought the same thing.

12

For several months Roy and Dale had been meeting with a newly formed Hollywood Christian Group, an organization originated by Henrietta Mears, director of Christian Education at the Hollywood Presbyterian Church. Regularly in attendance were Roy's longtime Sons of the Pioneers friend Tim Spencer and his wife Velma, Jane Russell, Connie Haines, Porter Hall, and many others.

It was, in fact, at one of the group's meetings that Roy first publicly gave his Christian witness. And it was there that he and Dale met guest speaker Billy Graham, who would invite them to join him for a crusade to be held in Houston's massive Rice Stadium.

Art Rush juggled their demanding schedule to clear the way for them to accept the popular evangelist's invitation. But it soon became clear that the only way they would be able to make it would be to fly to Houston, rather than make the trip by train as was their general habit.

The fear of flying which Dale had brought with her on her very first trip to Hollywood had remained and, in fact, grown worse after Robin's birth. Aware of her daughter's numerous needs, Dale had vowed never to board an airplane while Robin was living for fear she might be killed in a crash and thus leave her baby without a mother.

It was for that reason that she told Billy Graham she could not accept his invitation.

Though Roy and I both had come to a point where we accepted the condition and eventual fate of our little daughter, we felt it only right that we continue to seek ways to make her life as happy and normal as possible. We were no longer looking for miracles, but we didn't for a minute quit seeking help.

For instance, I had been made aware of a pediatrician in San Francisco who had reportedly done wonders with Mongoloid children in group therapy sessions, so I took Robin to see him. Like all those I had visited with before, he was frank. He suggested some glandular extracts and vitamins which might help improve her appetite and muscle tone, but said there was nothing he or anyone else could do about her heart condition.

Each time I was told something of that nature, I was more certain that my place was near her, my responsibility to remain at home. I stubbornly held to my conviction, despite the urging of Roy and Tim Spencer that I reconsider Billy Graham's offer to fly to Houston and witness to forty-five thousand people. None of those forty-five thousand, I was convinced, needed me nearly so much as did Robin.

And there were the other children to consider also. Dusty was having some problems in school, and Cheryl, growing into a young woman, was suddenly expressing an interest in knowing more about who her real mother and father were. I built a strong case: there were simply too many things at home which needed my attention. Roy would have to make the trip to Houston alone, despite his repeated attempts to persuade me to accompany him.

So it was that I drove him to the airport and then returned home, where I would spend a sleepless night.

By dawn I had come to a decision, one I had great difficulty arriving at but one which, when finally made, gave me great comfort. Roy and I had long said that Robin was God's child. From the day she was born, she had been more in his hands than ours. Thinking of these things, it finally occurred to me that my place was in Houston with my husband and Billy Graham and those thousands of people to whom we could witness.

I called Tim Spencer to tell him I had decided to fly to Houston. En route I would stop over in Dallas and get my

brother Hillman to drive me to Italy to see my father, who
was recovering from a stroke. And maybe I could visit the
administrator of Hope Cottage, where Cheryl had been
adopted, and see what advice she had to offer about Cheryl's
desire to find her real parents.

As I boarded the plane, it occurred to me that I was not
leaving Robin behind: I was taking her with me. I would tell
the people gathered in Rice Stadium of the things she had
brought to our home—the new understanding, the tolerance,
the kind of love which binds a family closer together.

Long before I even made it to Houston, I was glad I had
decided to make the trip. Dad, though still bedridden, seemed
to be doing better, and it was good to see the family. With
my sister-in-law I went to Hope Cottage in Dallas to discuss
Cheryl's problem. While there we were given a tour of the
home, and looked at many of the young children—most of
them no more than a couple of months old—who were residing
there, waiting to be adopted.

I went from crib to crib, looking at all those beautiful babies,
wishing I could pick each and every one of them up and hold
it. There was one in particular to whom my heart went out,
a little two-month-old girl with large brown eyes, beautiful olive
skin, and straight black hair. A strong, healthy baby, she was
already holding her head up well and was full of energy. I
thought as I looked down on her that she was the exact opposite
of my Robin.

She was, one of the cottage administrators told us, part
Choctaw Indian, part Scottish, part Irish, and her name was
Mary. Although it was against the rules, I asked and was allowed
to hold her for a moment. The big smile she gave me made
it hard to leave, but it was time for me to get to the airport.

I HAVE NEVER been prouder of my husband than I was as he
walked to the microphone in Rice Stadium in Houston. His
testimony, given in a down-home, straightforward manner,
brought tears to my eyes:

"Dale worked with God to bring me something I had longed
for all my life," he said. "Peace. Materially speaking, for years
I had nothing. Then for years I had much. But I soon learned

that having too much is worse than having too little. Nothing ever seemed quite right. I was restless, confused, unsatisfied. But the power of prayer, and the feeling of spiritual blessedness, and the love of Jesus have no price tags."

He went on to describe the strength he gained through daily Bible reading and prayer, and closed by denying published rumors that he was thinking of leaving show business and becoming an evangelist. "If I'm going to be an evangelist," he smiled, "I guess I'll have to do it on horseback, because being a cowboy is all I know."

Then it was my turn. For the first time, I mentioned Robin's illness publicly, telling of the shock and outrage we had first experienced and the understanding to which we had come with the help of God through Christ. Standing there on the floor of that giant football stadium, I was, quite needless to say, glad I had made the trip.

THE SUMMER OF 1952 was like an unending ride on a merry-go-round for the Roy Rogers family. We went from taping radio shows to shooting the new TV series to cutting records for RCA and back again. I found it very hard to believe that just a few months earlier we had all been sitting around wringing our hands over the fact that Roy had left Republic. As August approached, the only way he could have been involved in anything more would have been for there to have been two of him—and of me.

In addition to everything else, we were rehearsing and selecting wardrobes and generally tending to the myriad details that would need ironing out before we went to New York in September for a performance in Madison Square Garden.

And Robin would soon be celebrating her second birthday. August twenty-sixth was the only block on our kitchen calendar which did not have one or more commitments penciled in. There had, in fact, almost been an oversight; a press luncheon to give the new radio and TV series a traditional show-biz sendoff had almost been set on Robin's birthday. But we caught it in time and had it rescheduled for the Sunday evening prior to the family celebration we were planning.

When the schedule was made, we had no idea how traumatic

that day would wind up being. Cheryl came down with the mumps and, despite our care to keep Robin isolated, she caught them too. Her condition was soon complicated by encephalitis, and by late Saturday afternoon her temperature had risen to one hundred six. The doctor explained that the high fever had reached her brain, causing her tremendous pain.

The solemn look on the doctor's face struck fear in me. "I hate to tell you this," he said, "but as a doctor it is my obligation. The child's heart has undergone a considerable strain. It may not be able to stand the strain much longer. I can't tell you exactly what will happen or when it will take place, but it might be a good idea for you and Roy to prepare yourselves."

We sat up with her until past midnight, praying, trying to offer whatever comfort we could to her suffering. Finally, at the nurse's urging, we went into the house to try to rest. The idea of sleep seemed ridiculous to me.

At some point in the night it occurred to Roy and me that the elaborate press party had been scheduled for the following afternoon at the Brown Derby. It was too late to call it off, yet neither of us had any intention of leaving Robin. Finally I persuaded Roy to just drop by, put in a brief appearance, and then hurry back home.

Thus it would be a morning of unreal scenes: the other children, aware though uninformed about the gravity of the situation, sitting around the breakfast table and praying that God would spare their little sister, and Roy, pale and sadfaced, dressed in his King of the Cowboys splendor to make a public appearance he dreaded more than any he had ever made.

Despite everything we tried to do for her, Robin's fever continued to climb. By late afternoon on Sunday it had reached one hundred eight, and she had lapsed into unconsciousness.

By the time Roy returned, I had prayed every prayer I knew. I had prayed for some miracle that might spare my baby. But I released her to God about four o'clock in the evening, and prayed for an end to her pain, and for understanding and the strength to accept what was to be. And I cried more than I had ever cried before in my life. The tears were useless, but there was nothing else I could do—nothing else, really, that anyone could do.

Shortly after Roy returned, the nurse came through the door of Robin's little house and walked toward us. The words she would whisper were unnecessary; her face spoke them for her.

"She's gone," she said.

I COULD NOT BEAR to see Robin in death. No amount of human strength or persuasion could have gotten me to enter her little house before the ambulance arrived to take her. I wanted to remember her alive, with that angelic smile on her face.

And so it was that, while I grieved, the responsibility of the funeral arrangements fell to Roy. For the first time in our married life I was of no help to him. He shouldered the burden alone, selecting her white christening dress with the blue satin sash for her to be buried in. Around her neck he had placed a chain with a small gold cross that was to have been her birthday present.

Though I accompanied him to Forest Lawn to see that all the arrangements for the funeral had been tended, I refused flatly when he suggested that I come in with him and look at Robin. Feeling very near a nervous breakdown, I had no trust in my emotions. I simply didn't feel I could stand to see my beautiful baby no longer alive. Roy, who had already agreed to my request that the casket remain closed during the funeral until I had left the church, touched my hand and said he would be back in a few minutes.

When he returned, there was a strange look of peace on his face. For the first time since Robin's death, he didn't look tired and emotionally taxed. "That," he said as he got in the car, "was the hardest thing I've ever had to do, Dale, but I'm glad I did. The minute I looked at her I knew for certain she's with the Lord. She looked like a small sleeping angel."

The funeral was brief and simple. Dr. Harley Smith, who had baptized Robin, opened the service with a prayer. Dr. Jack MacArthur delivered a short sermon, and Leonard Eilers, the chaplain of our Hollywood Christian Group, gave the closing prayer after an organist had played several of our favorite hymns.

And so, with a funeral service instead of a party on her second birthday, the earthly life of Robin Elizabeth Rogers was over. As time would pass, I would become more and more aware of the magnificent things she had accomplished during her brief visit.

ON A NUMBER OF OCCASIONS following the public disclosure of Robin's condition, magazines had asked Dale to write a story about how she and her husband had dealt with the situation. Though no longer hesitant to tell the story of her child, Dale had repeatedly told editors that she would write the story only when she felt the time was right.

Soon after Robin's death, the urge to set the events of Robin's life to writing struck, and virtually every spare minute Dale had was spent in recording her thoughts and feelings about her child. She worked long into the night, between rehearsals and in the early morning hours before the rest of the family awoke. She wrote with an obsession—on legal pads, the backs of envelopes, scraps of paper—trying to link her words and thoughts in a manner she felt necessary.

But it wasn't working. "I knew what I wanted to say," Dale recalls, "but I just didn't know how to say it. Then one afternoon, as Roy and I were doing a radio broadcast, I had a few moments away from the mike to rest. I sat down, closed my eyes, and prayed. And suddenly there was this voice telling me, 'Let Robin write it. Let her speak for herself. You just be the instrument.'"

With new direction Dale's efforts went far beyond the length of a magazine article. It would, she had decided, be a book—Robin's book.

ROY, SEARCHING FOR WAYS to lift my spirit, suggested that we leave for our Madison Square Garden Rodeo engagement early, and stop in Texas for a few days' visit with my parents. Feeling emotionally and physically drained, I agreed that it was a good idea. Had I stopped to think, I would have recognized that there was more to my husband's plans than a few days of rest and relaxation and family reunion.

There was, it seemed, no way to get away from the sorrow that I was having such a difficult time overcoming. Our route to the train station went past Forest Lawn, and the sight of the brilliant cross lighted atop the chapel where Robin's funeral service had been held was more than I could take. For the first time in several days, I again broke into tears.

Thereafter, however, the trip went smoothly. After a while I handed some of the pages I had been writing to Roy, asking that he read them and tell me what he thought about the idea of my taking them to a publisher when we got to New York. He read the manuscript slowly, saying nothing. Once finished, he sat it in his lap and turned to look at me for the first time since he had begun to read.

"You had help," he said.

"Yes," I replied, "I had a lot of help."

Roy agreed that finding a publisher for the little book I planned to title *Angel Unaware* would be one of the major priorities while in New York.

On the final day of our visit with my family in Italy, Roy seemed unusually eager to make the drive to Dallas, where we would catch the train for New York. As we were preparing to leave, his motive finally surfaced. "Do you suppose," he said nonchalantly, "that little Indian baby you saw at the Hope Cottage is still there?"

I could read him like a book. Perhaps adopting a child would help to ease the pain of losing Robin. I made little effort to encourage his plan, pointing out that I had been told there were some people already interested when I had first seen the child. "I'm sure she isn't still available," I said, "but if you would like to stop by, that's fine with me."

My shoulder-shrugging casual front fell to pieces the minute I saw her again. As we walked toward her she held out her fat little hands and smiled. Suddenly I was the one who could be read like a book. I wanted that baby so badly I ached.

"Are you sure?" Roy asked.

"I'm positive."

"Well, he said, a big smile breaking across his face, "if we can work it out I'm all for it."

There was, we were told, a woman in Dallas who had expressed some interest in adopting Mary, but our request would be taken under consideration. The officials at Hope Cottage agreed to call us in New York if it appeared that things might work out for our adopting the beautiful little three-quarters Choctaw Indian girl.

The thought of our being able to have Mary and the need I felt to find a publisher for my book were the only things that kept me going in New York. Though I realized the responsibility of an entertainer to the public, it was a chore for me to get through every performance. I like to think I have some degree of acting talent, but putting on a happy face during that particular time in my life was no small task.

It seemed that complications bred additional complications. Though we called several times, the people at Hope Cottage had no answer for us. And I was fast learning that the publishing business is perhaps even tougher than show business.

Having read Dr. Norman Vincent Peale's book, *A Guide to Confident Living,* and gaining much from it, I made up my mind before even arriving in New York to see him about my book. Though his schedule was filled solidly for the next two weeks, he agreed to see me. I read it to him there in his office, and was overjoyed when he said he liked it and suggested I take it to his publisher, Prentice-Hall. I thanked him for his help, and wasted little time making the trip across the George Washington bridge to Englewood Cliffs, New Jersey, where Prentice-Hall was headquartered.

They turned it down, saying that it would conflict with a current book about a handicapped child, and that the reading public didn't want to cry. I didn't want to make anyone cry, or laugh, or sing with Robin's story. I simply wanted them to understand, to realize that there were four million children in the United States alone who would never know the joy of growing to adulthood, but that with love and help and understanding and proper rehabilitation, some were capable of advancing to a point where they could be productive and take care of themselves.

I took the book to a second publisher, and it was again rejected. With that rejection my faith began to slip. I began to question my purpose in having written the book, and to wonder if there really was anyone who cared about it's message.

Roy, dealing with problems of his own, urged me to not

give up, to remain patient. The battle he was fighting was with the management of Madison Square Garden. Having been advised that we planned to include a religious number in our performance, they called a committee meeting to discuss the situation. The 1952 World's Championship Rodeo, they decided, was not the proper place for religion.

They argued and pleaded, warning Roy and me that to do a religious number would be professional suicide. Even several merchants who sold various products of Roy Rogers Enterprises expressed their concern. Telling a crowd of kids in Houston, Texas, that they should go to church was one thing, but trying to bring religion to the world's biggest and most publicized rodeo in New York City was quite another. They simply could not allow it, for their sake and for ours.

To which Roy replied, "Dale and I have talked this thing out. If we can't do our religious number, we won't go on at all. We'll just head on back to California tonight." Grandstand plays have never been a trick of Roy's, yet in this situation it was the best weapon he had available. It worked.

At the appointed moment that evening, the jam-packed Garden went dark, with only the spotlights forming a huge cross in the center of the arena. And out of that beautiful darkened hush came Roy's voice, sounding better to me than ever before, singing "Peace in the Valley."

The forty-three performances we did over a period of twenty-six days broke all attendance records at the Garden. Because of Roy's record-breaking appearances over a period of eight years he was inducted into the Madison Square Garden Hall of Fame. And, to steal briefly from Art Rush's list of facts and figures about Roy's career, Roy Rogers once earned the Garden a one-day gross of one hundred nineteen thousand dollars. That same week Frank Sinatra grossed eighty-four thousand dollars for a seven-day appearance at the Palace just a few blocks away. Need I say more?

The success of our appearances, however, did little to lift my own spirits. The thought of going from publishing house to publishing house, only to hear polite turndowns, was unbearable to me. "Give it another chance," Roy kept saying. It was something I had to think about.

I went over to Central Park and sat alone on a bench for a long time, trying with little success to determine what my next step should be. Finally, I prayed to God to give me direction, to somehow make me aware of whether the pursuit was something I should go on with or something I should simply forget about. Sitting there with my eyes closed, I prayed for quite some time.

When I looked up, there before me stood a Mongoloid child about six years old, harnessed to a nearby nurse. That child was my sign. It would take more than two rejections to make me give up.

There would, for that matter, be no further rejections. That same afternoon, I received a call from Dr. Frank Mead, editor-in-chief at Fleming H. Revell Company. Someone at Abingdon Press, the second publisher to reject the book, had called him and suggested it might be something he would like to have a look at.

He was leaving that day for Chicago, he told me, and would like to take my manuscript along to read on the train. After having read it, he promised, he would call to let me know what he thought.

When he arrived in Chicago he phoned to tell me the wonderful news that he wanted to publish it. "I think," he added, "that it would be quite appropriate to set the publication date for the week of Easter."

That was to be just the beginning of the good news, however. Later in that same week, we finally got the call from Hope Cottage telling us that Mary was ours, that we had a new baby to pick up en route home.

Roy reacted like a youngster on Christmas morning. "We'll call her Mary Little Doe," he said. And then he called home. It was our plan to be home by October twenty-eighth for Dusty's birthday. "Son," Roy excitedly told him, "we're bringing you the greatest birthday surprise you could ever imagine."

It wound up being a bigger—and more wonderful—surprise than even I could have imagined.

I AM NOT EXAGGERATING when I say this entire book could be filled with anecdotes about the things Roy has done for children.

Sick ones, lonely ones, poor ones have received calls from him, personal visits in hospital rooms, or invitations to the ranch for the weekend.

One night, after a long and tiring show, we returned to our hotel and I immediately fell into bed. The next morning I awoke early as I usually do and found Roy gone. As the day wore on and I had no word from him, I began to get concerned and, in fact, considered placing a call to the local authorities for their help in locating him. But in the late afternoon, shortly before our performance, he showed up, apologizing for having been gone so long. My anger would hurriedly disappear when he told me where he had been.

He had been made aware of a five-year-old girl who, in a tragic gasoline explosion, had lost all her limbs. The girl's fondest wish was to be able to see one of our shows. So Roy had driven two hundred miles to issue the invitation in person, visiting with the child and her parents and making them aware that they had three reserved seats for the next evening's performance.

That night the mother brought her smiling little girl in a wicker laundry basket so she could see Roy perform.

And I'll never forget a little boy in Seattle named Rusty Rogers—no relation—who was in the hospital for what doctors thought to be leukemia and who simply refused to follow doctor's orders about proper rest and diet. In desperation, the father phoned, explaining the problem. In turn, Roy called Rusty's doctor and then placed a call to Rusty. He made a deal with him: if he would follow the doctor's orders and get well and strong again Roy would have him brought to the ranch for a weekend and let him ride Trigger. Rusty not only made that visit and rode Trigger, but years later was a surprise guest, very much alive, very healthy, on Ralph Edward's "This Is Your Life" show done with Roy. Ralph later said, "In all the years we did that show, the single person whose life we got more requests to do than any other was Roy Rogers."

The stories, as I said, could go on and on. Suffice it to say that my cowboy hero husband has always had a special feeling for the underdog, especially if that underdog happens to be very young and very fragile.

Following our closing performance in Madison Square Garden, the plan for our return home called for several stops along the way to do one-night performances. When we arrived in Cincinnati toward the end of the tour, Roy picked up the regular stack of letters and messages which always awaited him at every stop, and first opened a telegram from a woman who ran a welfare home for handicapped children, in nearby Covington, Kentucky and whose own little girl, Penny, had suffered from cerebral palsy since birth. The woman asked if it would be possible for her to come to Cincinnati, so Penny could see Roy and Trigger.

That evening Roy called her to say he would pay all the expenses if she would, indeed, bring her daughter to the following evening's show. In the course of the conversation Roy learned that she and her husband were, at the time, caring for seventeen children who were wards of the state, all unadoptable cases.

I could see Roy's eyes dancing as the conversation went on.

"You wouldn't happen to have a little boy there, say, about six, would you?" he asked.

She said that she did, but that he was slightly handicapped.

"Bring him with you," Roy said.

The show had already begun when our visitors from Covington arrived backstage. During intermission Roy went over and said hello to Penny, and then looked down at the young boy he had requested be brought along. He was peeking at Roy from behind the skirt of his foster mother, bashful and scared. "Hey," Roy said, "come over here for a minute."

The little boy summoned his courage and walked to Roy. The boy stood for a moment, then extended his hand and, in his best shoot-em-up drawl, said, "Howdy, pad-nuh."

"Howdy yourself," Roy said. He was hooked.

Later that night we sat in the hotel talking about this little boy, whose name was Harry. He had been abandoned twice, we had been told, and had suffered rickets and a slight curvature of the spine as a result of malnutrition. His nose had been broken, and his body bore evidence of mistreatment of the worst kind as an infant. And on top of all that, he had had a miserable cold when we met him.

Dusty, Roy pointed out, needed a companion. Long into the night we discussed whether this little boy, with all his problems, would be the answer. We frankly admitted to each other that it was, in some respects, a frightening proposition, but . . .

It was three in the morning when Roy rose from the couch and said, "Dale, anybody can adopt a perfect child." Thus, at three A.M., he placed a call to the foster home and asked how long it would take to get adoption proceedings underway for Harry. "We are on a tight schedule and will be leaving town tomorrow," he explained.

"Mr. Rogers," the surprised and delighted woman said, "if you will meet me at the courthouse at eight o'clock, I think we can pull enough strings to get you and Harry out of town on schedule."

In what may well be the fastest adoption on record, Harry, whom we had decided to call Sandy, was officially a member in good standing of the Rogers family by nine that morning. The proceedings were but a formality. There were no objections voiced by anyone. Anyone, that is, but Sandy. Before he was willing to go, he had to be satisfied that someone at the foster home would carry on his personal job there, the feeding of an older child who was suffering from meningitis.

We made a quick stop to buy him a new pair of jeans and a cowboy shirt to wear on the bus, and then Roy proudly carried him aboard and introduced the members of the troupe to his new son.

A whole new world filled with attention-giving adults suddenly opened up to Sandy on that bus ride. He soon put his shyness aside and was eager to get acquainted with everyone. He had brought his belongings with him in an unopened paper sack, and when someone asked what he had in it he smiled and proudly dug out the only article of clothing he owned—a far-worse-for-the-wear sweater.

There was more than one sudden clearing of the throat heard in the bus.

I loved him already.

WITH THE TOUR OVER, Roy, Sandy, and I flew to Dallas to pick up the other new member of our family, Mary Little Doe, whom I was already calling Dodie as if we had been lifelong friends.

And so we arrived in Los Angeles, as promised, on Dusty's birthday. All the kids were there to greet us. There was great excitement, much laughing and hugging for several minutes, and then Roy nudged me to get my attention. He nodded in the direction of Dusty and Sandy, who were standing facing each other but keeping their distance. Sandy, still a bit perplexed by the whole sequence of events which had brought him to this point, stood smiling. Dusty, on the other hand, was square-jawed, giving his new brother a very careful looking over.

"Don't worry," Roy said, "it'll work out. They'll be pals before you know it."

Frankly, it wasn't something that I was worried about. At that particular moment, with my family gathered around me, I was too happy to worry.

13

IF EVER THERE WERE QUESTIONS about the effect switching from motion pictures to television would have on the careers of Roy Rogers and Dale Evans, they were quickly and positively answered when the first rating polls were conducted. If anything, the weekly thirty-minute NBC episodes broadened Roy's and Dale's audience considerably.

Now it was no longer just the youngsters who were following their Western heroics, but entire families seated in living rooms across the country. To mom and dad, they were refreshing— a team whose show was not only entertaining but also taught their children high morals and made them aware of the high price of wrongdoing. To the kids, they were still Roy and Dale,

*good always triumphing over evil with a song and a smile or
two along the way.*

And rather than voicing displeasure over the fact that their
cowboy hero was married to his leading lady, youngsters began
looking up to Roy and Dale as the kind of parents every kid
would like to have. On at least a dozen occasions over the
years, misguided and frightened runaways appeared at their
California doorstep, suggesting that Roy and Dale might prove
to be better parents than those they had recently run away
from. In each instance, it took only a brief heart-to-heart talk
with the King of the Cowboys to reunite the strayed youngsters
with their distraught parents.

In addition to widespread public appreciation, Roy and Dale
received recognition from their peers; they were chosen 1953's
Best Actor and Best Actress in a network Western series.
Clearly, Republic's loss was television's gain.

"The Roy Rogers and Dale Evans Show" would, in the course
of its long run, establish itself as one of television's most successful—and most unique—efforts. From 1951 through 1958, it
was a weekly feature on NBC, under the sponsorship of General
Foods. For the next two and one-half years, it would be shown
in syndication, sponsored by Nestle's chocolate. Then, with Ideal
Toy Company joining forces as a co-sponsor alongside Nestle's,
the series was sold to CBS, where it would run for yet another
four years.

Roy and Dale's public appearance schedule was as demanding as it was lucrative, and always mixed with their songs and
variety acts was their message of Christian faith. Promoters,
no longer wary, knew full well that their headline attractions
were going to bring their religion to the stage with them. "I
think," says Art Rush, "that people finally realized that customers were as eager to see them perform as ever, but they were
also eager to hear and learn of Roy and Dale's faith in God.
All I know is that they set new attendance records wherever
they appeared."

This is not to say that Roy and Dale's performances were
ever lacking in fun and laughter. If nothing else, Trigger alone
saw to that.

On a trip to Hawaii for a series of performances, Roy had

the talented palomino sent over by boat in the company of trainer Glenn Randall several days after Roy, Dale, and the children had enjoyed a brief vacation. At the dock, Trigger was given a celebrity's welcome, complete with band, photographers, the customary leis, and native girls dancing the hula in their grass skirts. Trigger, delighted to be back on solid ground, and evidently ready to eat, promptly caused a roar of laughter by taking a healthy bite out of one of the dancing girls' skirts.

"He was," says Roy, "always the biggest ham in the family."

The early fifties, then, were good times for the Rogers family. Their two additional children added new meaning to their lives and, though hardly forgotten, the loss of Robin was turning from painful memories into warm reflections.

Dale's book was published in 1953 and by the end of the year had climbed to number three on the list of best-selling non-fiction books, trailing only the Revised Standard Version of the Bible and Norman Vincent Peale's The Power of Positive Thinking. *In the first two years alone four hundred thousand copies of* Angel Unaware *would be sold.*

And as the sales mounted, Dale announced that all royalties earned by the book would be donated to the National Association for Retarded Children.

While these were busy times, they were also times of enjoyment. Roy, always an enthusiastic outdoorsman, found time for occasional hunting and fishing trips, and for shooting trap and skeet at the Agua Sierra Gun Club with friends Robert Stack, Richard Crenna, and Clark Gable.

"The finest gun I ever owned," Roy says, "was one I bought from Clark Gable for six hundred and fifty dollars. One afternoon he was having a terrible time—couldn't hit anything. Finally, he turned around and said, 'Anyone want to buy this so-and-so?' I took him up on it before he had a chance to cool off and change his mind. I shot my first twenty-five targets straight the very next day."

The best times, though, came as Roy and Dale watched the kids grow.

DALE AND I HAD TOLD DUSTY that we were bringing Dodie home with us, but Sandy was a complete surprise. All the way home, Sandy talked a mile a minute, excitedly getting to know his new family, while Dusty remained very quiet.

The following morning Dale looked in on the boys and found Dusty busily hiding all of his toys before going off to school. He explained that he didn't want to come home later in the day and find that "that new guy" had made off with any of them.

That, of course, didn't last long. As soon as Dusty realized his new brother represented no threat to him, the toys came out and the two boys became fast friends—fast in every respect. What they didn't get into simply couldn't be gotten into.

One Saturday morning Dale looked outside to find them going from house to house, gathering up all the neighbors' mail so they could play postman. Exercising her "spare the rod and spoil the child" philosophy, she grabbed a switch and took off in hot pursuit. Now, my wife may be a fine actress, singer, and writer, but a track star she's not. It wasn't even a match. The punishment had to wait until the young partners in crime got hungry enough to come home.

We decided to keep Sandy out of school for a few months to allow him some adjustment time and to have doctors check on the physical problems we knew he had.

His coordination was poor—so poor that he was unable to ride the bicycle we bought for him. His breathing problems, we found out, were the result of a closed nostril. The surgeon who corrected the difficulty told us that it was obviously the result of an injury he had sustained as an infant, either from a fall or perhaps a blow from a fist. Sandy had a tremendous fear of even the slightest heights, and initially reacted to discipline by breaking into a sweat and getting sick to his stomach.

And then the doctors at the Los Angeles Children's Hospital did a series of tests which revealed abnormality in the brainwaves, an indication of slight brain damage. Sandy, they told us, would have what they termed plateaus of learning. He was not mentally retarded, but his mental and emotional development would be slow and at times difficult.

Difficult tasks, we would learn in years to come, brought out the best in Sandy Rogers. Maybe he had some problems; maybe he didn't move with the athletic grace of his brother; maybe it took him longer to do his lessons or learn a new skill, but he gave it everything he had—and you could see the warm look of self-satisfaction in his eyes with every new accomplishment, no matter how small.

After a while we sent him along with Dusty to attend second grade classes at a military school. He didn't exactly make the dean's list, but he worked hard and seemed to thoroughly enjoy school.

And Dusty made allowances. While he dealt Sandy a good measure of teasing and a normal amount of boyhood badgering, he seemed to recognize Sandy's difficulty with games and was far more patient than critical. As long as Sandy wanted to play, there was a spot for him. And if anyone took it upon himself to give Sandy a hard time about striking out or dropping a pass, he had Dusty to deal with.

They were, believe me, fun to watch—fun and frustrating. They were living, breathing proof that boys will be boys.

Cheryl was fast growing into quite a young lady, and Linda was catching up with her older sister as fast as she could. And little Dodie enjoyed to the fullest all the advantages of being the baby of the family. An occasional case of the croup aside, she was as healthy and happy and normal a baby as you would ever hope to see.

It didn't take any Rhodes scholar to realize that we were truly blessed. If I had it to live all over again, though, I would just as soon Dusty and Sandy hadn't sneaked into the garage and methodically peeled all the rubber off the dashboard of my racing boat.

OUR FAMILY wasn't the only thing that was thriving.

The membership of the Hollywood Christian Group had grown steadily to the point of having its own headquarters, operated by Tim and Velma Spencer. The doors were kept open day and night for prayer and counsel, and on Monday evenings we held our regular meetings at various members' homes.

Billy Graham was the guest speaker at a meeting which was held in the backyard of our home. He told of being invited to conduct a Crusade for Christ in London, and was having trouble deciding whether to accept the invitation or not, since the invitation had been extended by just a few churches. I asked him if there was anything Dale and I could do to help. We had a sizable fan club in the British Isles, I explained, and would be more than glad to do whatever we could.

He smiled and, half kiddingly, said, "You weren't planning on being over there in the early spring, were you?"

"We will if it will help," I said.

THAT'S THE KIND of careful planning that drives Art Rush up the wall. Even before Billy left our home, I had explained the situation to Art, and he had immediately gone about the chore of rearranging schedules and laying the groundwork for us to do our first overseas tour, winding up in London's giant Wembley Stadium, where we would join Graham's crusade in its seventh week.

The theaters were all sold out even before we left the States. We opened our tour in Glasgow and proceeded on to Edinburgh, Birmingham, and Liverpool, then on to Belfast and Dublin. We enjoyed the countryside and the people along the way, although we were disturbed to read in the British press that Graham's visit was being dealt sarcastic and downright cruel treatment by many leading spokesmen of the British media. Generally, the press was friendly to us, but there were times they let their suspicions show. And on at least one occasion, they got their facts a bit jumbled . . .

While we were already in Scotland, Mary Jo and Art were en route aboard the Queen Mary. One evening a wire reached Art, informing him that I had been shot during a performance in Glasgow. Art went into a panic and pressured the ship's wireless operator mercilessly to find out more details. After several hours of hand-wringing I knew nothing about, Art finally got the real story.

The opening scene of our stage show in Glasgow had called for our singing group, dressed as outlaws—neckerchief masks and all—to enter from stage right and to shoot blanks toward the opposite side of the stage, where I was to make my entrance on Trigger. It had been my responsibility to load all guns used in the show, including those for a shooting act later in the program which used live ammunition. By accident, I had loaded one of their guns with bird shot. I realized the error of the load as the "outlaws" began to shoot; I felt Trigger flinch and noticed several burning places on my face and in my arms and legs. You know the show must go on; I went to the microphone with blood streaming down my face and said, "You know, they've been shooting at me for twenty years, and this is the first time they've hit me." I introduced the next act, and asked if there was a doctor in the house who would come backstage. After having a few bird shot picked out of us, Trigger and I went on with the show. We had a few hot spots for awhile, but found they were not nearly so damaging as the news had been to Art Rush on his ocean cruise.

When we reached Liverpool, Dale and I both came down with a galloping case of the European flu and were ordered to bed by a local doctor. A press conference had been scheduled for that afternoon, and there were writers who insisted to Art that they were convinced the flu story was nothing more than a carefully planned Hollywood ploy to get out of the interviews. And all the while we were being shot full of penicillin and sulfa and feeling like we would have to get better to die.

Gradually it turned into a circus. A couple of journalists finally succeeded in sneaking into our room and actually put their hands on our foreheads to see if we really were running a fever. Outside, a crowd of something in the neighborhood of twenty thousand had gathered, chanting for us to come out and sing a couple of songs. At that particular moment I couldn't have hummed "Mary Had a Little Lamb," and Dale was having a worse time of it than I was.

Finally the crowd was appeased when our singing group, the Whip-O-Wills, along with Trigger, put on a brief performance in the street in front of the hotel. Believe me, there's more truth than poetry to the old axiom that there's no business like show business!

All in all, however, the trip was an enjoyable experience. The crowds were great, the countryside beautiful, and the people warm and friendly.

There was one particular person we met while visiting in an Edinburgh orphanage called Dunforth who particularly impressed us. Her name was Marion Fleming, a tiny little girl with a beautiful voice. She sang "Who Will Buy My Pretty Flowers?" for us, and I thought Dale was going to grab her up on the spot and make a run for the door.

Instead, however, we asked if it would be okay for her to join us for lunch at our hotel later. We were so taken by her that we invited her to come to California to visit with us the following summer, as soon as her school was out.

English law forbids Americans' adopting children whose parents are still living without the parents' permission, and even then the adoptive parents have to reside two years in Britain. Marion's parents were divorced, so the matron of the orphanage said a summer visit would be the best arrangement she could make. But that summer visit was later extended through Christmas, and even longer when finally we officially became Marion's guardians.

"Roy," Dale once said to me, "we're either going to have to stop visiting orphanages or buy us a hotel to live in."

The apprehensions everyone had felt about London and Billy Graham's crusade were gone by the time we appeared with him in the seventh week of his crusade. Preaching with a power that can only be divinely inspired, he not only captivated the crowds but quickly began to win over the skeptical members of the press. The same writers who were describing him as a preacher who looked more like a Madison Avenue television salesman were soon singing his praises.

By the time the crusade came to a close, there were ninety thousand people standing in the rain in Wembley Stadium to hear him preach. As he spoke with that booming, forceful voice, spreading his message to a crowd which seemed not at all perturbed by the weather, the Archbishop of Canterbury held an umbrella for him.

For Billy Graham, the crusade was an unquestionable success. For Roy Rogers and Dale Evans, it was an experience never to be forgotten. Our spirits, already lifted by the success of the tour and the crusade, rose even higher at the thought of getting back home. The television series was still several episodes behind the hurried-up shooting schedule we had gone through prior to our trip, and I was eagerly looking forward to some hunting and fishing and spending some time with the kids.

Art Rush, the man who never sleeps, had other plans. We were, he smilingly informed me, scheduled for a three-week tour that would carry us to Ohio, Indiana, Michigan, Missouri, Tennessee, and Texas. "Just think," he said, "you'll both get to work in your home states while we're gone."

I thought about mentioning that it would suit me just fine to work in my own backyard, but it would have done no good. I was just thankful he hadn't scheduled us to fly straight to Columbus, Ohio, from Wembley Stadium.

Just as we were preparing to go onstage in Columbus, I was called to the phone to take a long distance call. When the conversation was completed, the show had begun, and Dale was already onstage. When I took my place beside her at the mike, she immediately asked what the call had been about. I told her I would tell her after the show; I had decided to wait until we got back to the hotel to tell her the bad news which had been given me over the phone. Once there, I said, "Dale, I just got word that—" She did not allow me to complete the sentence.

"—my father is dead," she said. Dale says she has strange feelings before tragedy strikes. That night, she had been unaccountably nauseated before going onstage.

And so she was off to Texas to help her mother and brother in preparations for the funeral. I had planned to accompany her, but she argued against it. I had a contractual responsibility to complete the tour, she pointed out, and she would be all right. "You don't have to *go* with me to *be* with me, you know," she said. "I'll be fine."

I guess if we spend another thirty years together I'll still find myself amazed at the lady.

THE FOLLOWING SUMMER Cheryl decided it was high time for her first really big splash in show business. On numerous occasions she and the other kids had joined us onstage, but she had in mind something a bit nearer the spotlight.

So we took her with us for our appearance at the Canadian

National Exhibition in Toronto. I won't go so far as to say it was a mistake, but she did come down with a pretty serious case of show business fever. As a father, I didn't know whether to be proud or to go through the audience punching noses of all the young men who whistled and applauded her with such enthusiasm. Needless to say, Cheryl loved it, and matter-of-factly informed us that she was eagerly looking forward to the show we were scheduled to do in Madison Square Garden a month later.

It had come time to put a parental foot down. Dale and I both explained to her that to participate in the New York show would mean her missing the first several weeks of school, and that was completely out of the question. We got the whole mistreated teenager routine before we left, and had hardly unpacked after our arrival when a neighbor called to inform us that Cheryl had come to her, angrily announcing that she was leaving home forever.

To her everlasting credit, the neighbor had already called Father Smith at St. Nicholas, knowing that Cheryl held him in high regard, and he came over to discuss the problem with her. For a few days, it seemed as if we were talking long distance every minute we weren't working.

Father Smith, working in the role of a gentle arbitrator, heard both sides of the issue, and finally suggested to us that it might be a good idea for Cheryl to be on her own for a while. He suggested enrolling her in a girl's school, recommending Kemper Hall in Kenosha, Wisconsin. He said he felt reasonably certain that Cheryl would agree to it, and suggested that the move be made immediately.

Addled by the whole series of events, we talked it over and came to the decision that the situation offered precious few alternatives. In her current frame of mind, Cheryl was not going to be happy at home regardless, and there was the disturbing possibility that if told to stay against her strong will, she might well go far beyond the neighbor's house the next time she decided to leave.

Father Smith tried to make things easier for us, agreeing to handle the details and pointing out that this sudden bid for independence by our oldest daughter was hardly original.

Welcome to the teenage years, he said, pointing out several similar cases he had dealt with which had come to happy endings. He insisted to us that, in his opinion, we were far from losing a daughter.

Okay, we finally said, let's give Kemper Hall a try.

As soon as we had completed our engagement in New York, Dale went to Kenosha to visit Cheryl and talk things over. In addition to the normal run of teenage problems she was wrestling with, she had developed a growing concern about her real mother. Dale, having a better understanding of such things, dealt with that particular aspect of the problem admirably. She promised that if Cheryl was still so inclined when she reached twenty-one, Dale would do everything possible to help her find her real mother. In the meantime, though, she would have to remain in school and see to it that her grades stayed high.

That following summer, she returned home with high marks in each of her subjects, and life went on in the Rogers household as if she had not even been away.

And I should point out here that Dale did keep her end of the bargain, helping Cheryl to find her real mother. Cheryl even went to her mother's home for a weekend visit, and evidently came home with answers to all her questions about her background.

One thing which Cheryl found upon her return from school was that we were again planning a move. Which was no big deal to her, inasmuch as we had bounced around like so many ping-pong balls since she was just a little baby. This time it was to a one hundred and thirty-eight acre ranch in Chatsworth.

It was the kind of place we had been talking about for quite some time. On the ranch was a beautiful old brick and frame house which could be made accommodating by simply having an addition built on to both ends of it.

The purpose of moving to a place with so much acreage was twofold. First, it would provide us with much needed elbow room and, second, we were planning to use the ranch as a handy location site for shooting movies and television specials. Soon after our move, in fact, the company which produced the TV series "Brave Eagle" came to do some filming, much to Dodie's horror.

One morning Dodie came frantically flying into the kitchen to inform Dale that a bunch of wild Indians were coming to get her. Looking outside, Dale saw a group of actors on horseback, fresh from makeup, dressed in full Indian regalia, wearing war paint and practicing blood-chilling war cries.

It was no easy task to convince our own little Indian that she was seeing nothing more than a bunch of grown men playing a game. Finally Dale took Dodie out and introduced her to some of the visiting actors to prove to her they had no intentions of scalping or kidnapping any little girls.

As our family grew together, Dodie found herself something of an odd-girl-out. Dusty and Sandy were like two peas in a pod, and Marion and Linda had become very close. Cheryl, of course, was too interested in boys to have need for a pal at home.

So it was that when Dr. Bob Pierce of World Vision, Inc. brought by some films he had taken showing the plight of Korean orphans who were the victims of racially mixed marriages, the germ of an idea was planted. Suddenly we were talking about making room for one more: maybe Dr. Pierce could find a little Korean girl about Dodie's age. We gave him a picture of Dodie, explaining our wishes to him, and he said he would see what he could do.

Meanwhile, we had plenty to keep us busy. There were times when Dusty and Sandy fully qualified to be known as the Terrible Twosome—like the time things began to turn up missing around the house. After a little detective work, helped along by a conversation with the principal at the Northridge Military Academy, we learned that they had a thriving business going at school, selling off little items they were certain would not be missed from home. When confronted, both readily admitted their transgressions and said they were fully prepared to accept the consequences. What they got was my best "thou shalt not steal" lecture and, as an added bonus, a good old fashioned bottom-busting out in the garage.

There are times, it seems to me, when words need a little action to go with them.

Then, just to keep things from getting boring, the house caught fire. I was away on a trip at the time and would get the full details only after arriving back home.

It was the Christmas season, and in decorating the house Dale had placed a large candle atop the television cabinet. One evening Marion was engrossed in a late movie and remained up after everyone else had gone to bed to see its conclusion. She had, of course, been reminded to blow the candle out before she too retired.

Sometime just before dawn Cheryl woke to find the television set already burned to ashes, the piano smoldering, and a huge hole burned almost through the living room floor. She calmly went to the phone and called the fire department, then went about the business of waking Dale and the rest of the children and getting them out of the house.

For a half-hour they all stood outside in a drizzling early morning rain, waiting for the fire truck to arrive while the living room, dining room, and kitchen were turning to black, charred ruins.

We celebrated that particular Christmas in our den, with the distinct smell of smoke mingling with evergreen and turkey and dressing.

WHILE WE WERE PERFORMING at the annual Houston Fat Stock Show and Rodeo, a letter arrived from Dr. Pierce. Along with it, he had sent a photograph of the little part Korean, part Puerto Rican girl he had selected from over six hundred possibilities as a companion for Dodie. The picture of three-year-old In Ai Lee, a very serious-faced, pretty little girl with a Dutch bob hairdo and soft brown eyes, was all the convincing we needed.

Dr. Pierce immediately set to work to clear her for adoption. By June, he told us, the Roy Rogers–Dale Evans League of Nations family would have an additional member.

I'll never forget that afternoon at the airport as he stepped off the plane carrying In Ai Lee—we had decided to call her Deborah Lee—in his arms. There was no hint of a smile on her little face, but as soon as I reached for her she came to me without the slightest hesitation.

From that moment on, Dale insists, she was "daddy's girl," and I find it hard even now to argue the fact. We just seemed to hit it off at once.

We were due at the studio shortly after Debbie's arrival, so we took her with us, everyone in the family taking turns trying to make her feel at ease and to coax a smile from her. Our failures were duplicated by the cast and crew, who did everything but stand on their heads to try to erase the serious look from her face. It occurs to me now that she probably thought we were all operating with something less than a full deck. But, whatever her judgment, she was having none of this smile-for-your-new-family business.

Until, that is, one of the cameramen came walking toward her with a big red balloon. That did it. Little Miss Stoneface burst into a wide grin as she accepted the present.

That obstacle behind us, we moved on to the Americanization of our newest daughter. It didn't take long to realize that it would not be an easy task. American balloons, for instance, were quite nice, but the beds Debbie could do without. For weeks Dale would tuck her into bed and return later to find her stretched out, sleeping soundly on the bare floor as had been her custom in her homeland. Though she had been taught a few words of English by the missionaries she had lived with for a time before coming to us, she held stubbornly to her native tongue. She would try to draw Dodie into a conversation, rattling off Korean a mile a minute, and little Dodie, five months her elder, would just shake her head and say, "I don't understand." Debbie would finally get one of those exasperated looks on her face and go back to whatever it was she had been doing before the one-sided conversation began.

And then one day, after a frustrating experience of trying to make Dale understand something and having her mother say that she didn't understand what she wanted, she placed her little hands on her hips, shrugged her shoulders, sighed deeply, and walked away. From that moment on she never spoke Korean again. She had made a brave effort and failed, so she evidently decided that when in America . . . In a month she was speaking English as plainly as Dodie.

Still, for some time to come, every day would bring a new

experience for her. For instance, the first time she ventured out of the house and was greeted by Bullet, she became hysterical. Bullet, the friendliest dog I ever owned, was more surprised than we were. Finally, it was explained to us that German shepherds were trained as police dogs in Korea to guard against looting. They were taught to be vicious, much as Dobermans are in this country, and to obey only their masters. Becoming a dog lover was no easy task for Debbie.

And it was with no small amount of hesitation that she accepted the large crowds which would greet us at airports and come to our performances. Crowds to her meant angry, violence-bent mobs, and there was real fear in her eyes before she was finally satisfied that the people had not come to do us any harm but, rather, came because they liked us.

It was exciting to watch her solve so many of life's mysteries, to see her gain in confidence with each new revelation. Life holds a great many pleasures to be sure, but I question whether there is any one more heart-warming, rewarding, and downright enjoyable as watching children grow.

You have to look fast, though, because they grow up in a hurry.

By the late 1950s, the Roy Rogers family was among the most well-known in America. Journalists were forever fascinated by the fact that Roy and Dale had adopted so many children, and were amazed at the manner in which they had so successfully mixed religion and the entertainment business.

Whenever school schedules would permit, Roy and Dale would take their family with them for personal appearances and ofttimes allowed them small parts in their act. Once the Roy Rogers–Dale Evans Show, it had evolved into Cheryl's doing a few numbers, then Linda and right on down the line. Dodie and Debbie, dressed like twins, did a sister act which became a favorite of the crowds.

Still, it was the King of the Cowboys and the Queen of the West whom people came to see. The remarkable string of attendance records they established at virtually every stop stood as testimony to the fact that their popularity had waned not in the least.

"They were so popular and such familiar faces," says Art Rush, "that it became all but impossible for them to go anywhere in the U.S. or in foreign countries and not be recognized.

"When Roy and Dale appeared at the Canadian National Exhibition in Toronto, Roy decided he wanted to see the fair grounds without being recognized. So he put on a fireman's uniform, dark glasses, and a fake beard and set out for his afternoon at the fair. He got about a hundred yards before someone came up to him and asked for an autograph and an explanation of why he was dressed up in such a ridiculous outfit.

"The tip-off, he later learned, was the fact that he had failed to take off the gold-tipped boots he had worn in his performance earlier in the day."

And while their popularity with adults continued to grow, hero-worshiping youngsters still formed the backbone of their audience. As part of a promotion of their appearance in Milwaukee one year, a small ad ran in the local paper telling the youngsters of the city that if they would call a certain number, they would have the opportunity to say hello to the King of the Cowboys. What they heard when they called was a tape recording of Roy's voice saying, "Howdy, partner. This is Roy Rogers . . ."

After over three hundred thousand calls, the local telephone company informed the promoters of the state fair that it would be necessary to suspend the calls before their circuits went completely haywire.

As entertainers Roy and Dale were touching virtually all the bases—major rodeos, state fairs, television, radio, records, live performances. And Dale's second book, My Spiritual Diary, was furthering her reputation as a writer with a unique gift.

If there was any aspect of their professional career which concerned Roy, it was the fact that the appellate court had, in 1954, reversed the decision in his suit against Republic Studios. While the decision came long after he and Dale had gained a strong foothold in the TV market, making it, for all practical purposes, a dead issue, Roy was genuinely disappointed at the lack of support he received from his peers in the motion picture business.

"Ronald Reagan was the president of the Screen Actors Guild at the time," Roy recalls, *"and when I went to him for help he told me there was nothing he could do. It became clear to me early that I was in my fight alone. And facing pretty bad odds."*

Indeed, one of the Republic attorneys later told Rush that every major studio in Hollywood had made their legal teams available to Republic during the drawn-out legal battle.

"There was a strong feeling within the industry," reflects Rush, *"that an outright victory by Roy would have spelled trouble for the movie business from then on with people under contract. Which was a bit absurd, particularly in the light of the fact that Roy was probably the only actor to have a clause in his contract giving him commercial rights to his name, voice, and likeness. He had no intentions of doing anything more than protecting his own rights.*

"But from that day to now he has not made a motion picture in this town. He says he was blackballed, and I have to agree with him."

To Roy Rogers, however, all that is water under a bridge he crossed long ago. Blackballed or not, it caused no serious damage to his career. If anything, it only channeled it in different directions.

14

WHEN THE ROGERS FAMILY made the move to Chatsworth, they found no Episcopal church. So they accepted the invitation of Dr. Harold Hayward to attend his local Methodist services, and quickly fell into enthusiastic involvement. The children were soon busy with Methodist Youth Fellowship and Vacation Bible School, and Roy and Dale became regulars at Sunday school and church services, with Dale and the older girls singing in *the choir. Dusty and Debbie were eventually baptized by Dr. Hayward—Dodie, Linda, and Sandy having been baptized at St. Nicholas Church in Encino.*

Problems later arose, however, after Roy and Dale partici- pated in a Christian Anti-Communist Crusade in Los Angeles's Shrine Auditorium, each giving a brief testimony. The crusade was conducted by Dr. Fred Schwarz, himself a former Commu- nist who had been converted to Christianity. And while many saw good in his work and willingly lent him support, he was labeled by some religious leaders and liberals as a rabble-rouser, a controversial figure the Christian faith could well do with- out.

The day after Dr. Schwarz's crusade, a Methodist Conference speaker at their church publicly denounced his efforts and strongly urged the congregation of the Chatsworth Methodist Church to have nothing to do with any form of anti-Communist movement.

It was quite clear which particular members of the Chatsworth congregation the directive was aimed toward.

Though urged to remain by many of the friends they had gained in the Methodist faith, Roy and Dale decided to leave the church before their own beliefs and convictions—which included a strong stance against godless Communism—created further problems within the church family. Quietly they moved their membership to the Chapel in the Canyon in nearby Ca- noga Park, an independent church with a Disciples of Christ background.

"It had been our plan," remembers Dale, "to visit several churches before placing our membership, but when we visited the Chapel in the Canyon and met its pastor, Larry White, when we saw the enthusiasm and love he had for the young people of the church, our search was over."

As always, young people—their own and others—were ma- jor concerns in the lives of Roy Rogers and Dale Evans. In the course of their lengthy and celebrated careers, many hon- ors have been bestowed upon them. One which Dale Evans most cherishes and Roy deems most deserved came in 1967, when Dale Evans Rogers was named California Mother of the Year.

ROY AND I BOTH went into a state of shock when Cheryl graduated from high school and announced that she was planning to marry. Things like that have a way of sneaking up on you. One day it's scratched knees and mud pies, and the next time you notice they're asking for permission to borrow the car and your opinion about their new shade of eye shadow. Personally, I think they do it with some kind of magic. You see them day in and day out, but aside from noticing that you have to buy clothes a size larger and stock the refrigerator with greater regularity, you still have a hard time realizing they are fast gaining on adulthood.

One of my favorite stories about the swiftness with which children grow up has to do with the husband and wife who are sitting at the breakfast table one morning, talking about their kids. The mother asks the father what he thinks they should do about enrolling their son in a driver's education course.

The father gives it little thought before saying, "There's no big rush. They won't let little kids drive cars anyway, you know."

"Honey," the mother pointed out, "your son is *not* a little kid any more. He's sixteen years old."

"Already?" the stunned father replied.

That's the way Roy and I felt when Cheryl began making plans for a Valentine's Day wedding to her sweetheart, Bill Rose. He was—and is—a fine young man, and we had no objections to the marriage (well, no more than any parents do when their daughter takes such a step). But I did make a token attempt to persuade her to give it a little more time and perhaps get a year of college behind her first.

I need not tell you how much good the wise old high school dropout did with that suggestion. She was married in a beautiful ceremony in St. Nicholas Church, with Linda serving as her maid of honor, Marion as a bridesmaid, and Dodie and Debbie as junior bridesmaids.

Doing it up in high style, she invited seven hundred and fifty to attend the wedding. I did all the things a mother is supposed to do: I poured punch, I laughed, I cried, and I felt a little older than I had in quite some time. And I delighted in the joy I saw in the faces of Cheryl and her new husband.

Then, just a month later, Marion too was gone, married to Dan Eaton, a marine stationed at nearby Camp Pendleton, in a small, quiet ceremony at the ranch.

Suddenly it seemed like a good time to take inventory, before we looked and the house was empty. Linda, into her teen years, was beginning to draw the same whistles of approval from the audience that Cheryl had. The boys, Dusty and Sandy, had finally eased out of what Roy liked to refer to as their knot-headed stage, and were doing well at the Ridgewood Military Academy. Even Debbie and Dodie were growing almost too fast to keep up with.

There were, quite clearly, no more babies in the Rogers household.

THE NEXT THING we knew Linda, though still in her early years of high school, was madly in love and steadily dating a fine young athlete at her school named Gary Johnson. Aware that the relationship was getting quite serious, Roy and I discussed it at length and came to the decision that enrolling her in Kemper Hall, where Cheryl had done so well, might be the best thing for her as well as for young Gary.

It wasn't one of the more popular decisions we've ever made. Linda didn't like it one iota but, to her everlasting credit, went away and made excellent grades. When she returned home in June, announcing that she was still very much in love with Gary and wanted to marry him, we knew full well the trip had not solved the problem.

It was time to again go to the bargaining table. Finish school, we urged, and we would see to it that she had whatever kind of wedding she wished, along with our wholehearted blessings. So four months later she and Gary eloped to Las Vegas and, with the groom's parents serving as witnesses, were married. When I got the news I was recovering from pneumonia and almost went into a relapse. Never mind that I had run off and gotten married much earlier, and had waited two days before even telling my parents where I was or what I had done. This was different. Well, I thought it was. After all, it was my first time on the other side of the fence.

I sat for a while, allowing the anger to advance to numbness and, finally, resignation. All I had to do then was call Roy, who was in New York, and break the news to him. While the elopement had come as a surprise to me, Roy's reaction didn't. I'm sure half of New York City heard the objection he yelled into the telephone after he had heard the news. He said he was heading home right away to straighten things out.

I didn't bother to tell him that there was nothing he could straighten out. Instead, I suggested he complete his business there and *then* come home. That, I knew, would provide him with a little cooling-off time before he returned to meet the new bride and groom.

As I've already pointed out, there is seldom a dull moment in the Rogers family.

WITH THE REGULAR ROUTINE of shooting movies and doing a weekly television series behind them, the professional pace of Roy Rogers and Dale Evans slowed somewhat in the 1960s. Which is not to say they had any great lapses of idle time. There was always another rodeo or state fair to attend, a TV special on which to make a guest appearance, or a religious function at which to give witness.

And while the head count at home had dwindled considerably, it wasn't long before there were grandchildren visiting the Rogers home.

"When our older kids were young," Dale reflects, "I think there were too many times that Roy and I had to be away. I regret that part of it. So does Roy. It just seemed there was always someplace we had to be, something we had to do. That's just one of the things you have to accept when you get involved in a business like ours.

"With so much travel, though, we were lucky that we worked together, rather than one of us filming a movie in Europe or somewhere while the other was busy on the other side of the world. I can imagine how hard it is for show business families which are constantly scattered in every direction.

"And, to be honest, I'm not saying I would do things much differently if I had it to do all over again. I'm reasonably certain I would probably jump right out and make a lot of the same stupid mistakes I did the first time around."

She and Roy both agree, however, that it was nice when the time finally came that there were occasional days on the calendar with no obligations penciled in.

THE FACT OF THE MATTER is, I think there came a time when Roy had too much free time—for motorcycle riding, speedboat racing, and all of those kinds of wonderful pursuits which kept me looking down toward the gate to see if he was coming home in one piece.

For instance, it has always been my opinion that the tremendous jarrings he took during his ocean speedboat racing for eight years were what ultimately made it necessary for him to enter the hospital in 1964.

For some time he had been complaining of severe pain in his neck. The doctor who examined him found that three vertebrae were jammed together because of worn discs and an operation would be necessary to correct the problem.

We had been planning a family vacation for some time, but the doctors insisted that Roy take things easy and be prepared for surgery as soon as possible. Roy agreed, but only after I promised that I would go on to Hawaii for a few days with the children.

Dusty liked the hula girls, Dodie and Debbie the beach and sail boats, and Sandy was captivated by every serviceman— sailor, soldier, marine—he met. Almost from his first day in the military academy, Sandy had been fascinated with anything that dealt with the military. His favorite toys as a child were tanks and minature jeeps. He would sit for hours on the floor in his room, maneuvering his troops and artillery around, fighting make-believe battles, and winning resounding victories.

I think there in Hawaii, talking with all those young men in uniform, he made the decision that he would enlist as soon as he reached the necessary age. But I really didn't give it much thought then; I was comfortable in the knowledge that he was still too young. And frankly, I had Roy's operation on my mind most of the time.

THE SURGERY, lasting nine long hours, went well, but unexpected complications set in a week later when Roy suffered a painful staph infection. That soon passed, however, and the day after

Debbie's twelfth birthday we were allowed to move him from the hospital to the quiet of a convalescent home in Bel Air.

Seeing her father on the mend was better than any birthday present Debbie received. She had worried mightily during his stay in the hospital, constantly coming to me for assurance that he was going to be okay and home soon.

She had always been daddy's girl, always the first to greet him on his arrival home, and delighted in sitting on his lap even when she had reached an age at which most girls find it "childish," combing his hair for him as he sat reading the paper or watching television.

When she realized that the move from the hospital to the convalescent home was a step toward Roy's return to the ranch, her spirits lifted greatly. No longer worried, her boundless energy returned, and she again became the tireless, exuberant young girl we had been watching with amazement for nine years. Nine years; it didn't seem possible that that much time had passed since Dr. Bob Pierce had stepped off that plane with her in his arms.

Even just a year earlier, at Youth Night during Billy Graham's Los Angeles Crusade, when she, Dodie, Dusty, and Sandy had rededicated their lives to Christ, she had looked to me like a little girl.

But no longer. Soon, it occurred to me, she too would be a young woman, anxiously looking ahead to the opportunity to make her own place in the world.

The Sunday following her birthday she sang in the choir and then joined her friends in a discussion of the next day's planned bus trip to Tijuana, where the young people of the church would deliver gifts to an orphanage.

It was a trip she had long looked forward to—and one I almost didn't allow her to make. During the Sunday services Dodie became ill, and since there might be need of Debbie's help at home the next day I told her the bus trip was out.

Naturally, she was crushed and pointed out to me that if she was not allowed to go her two best friends, Kathy and Joanne Russell, would not be allowed to make the trip. I gave in.

And the following morning she and her friends climbed aboard the gift-loaded bus, giggling, laughing, full of life; I went to the Bel Air Convalescent Home to spend the day with Roy.

Later that afternoon, as I drove home along the San Diego Freeway, I was lost in thought about a myriad things—Roy's recuperation, the children, things I wanted to do to the house—and didn't even bother to turn on the car radio. By not doing so I postponed briefly one of the most shocking, saddening moments of my life.

As soon as I pulled into the driveway I knew something was amiss. Ruth Miner, our housekeeper, waited patiently at the door while I parked the car and then quickly, silently took me by the arm and led me into the living room.

"Dale," she said, with a strange look on her face, "I have to talk to you." At the sound of her voice and the expression on her face my body tensed in foreboding. I could literally feel the blood draining from my face.

"The bus," she continued, tears building in her eyes, "had an accident after if left San Diego. Debbie and Joanne Russell are with the Lord."

With the Lord? For a split second it failed to sink in. Then the realization struck like a blow from a hammer. She was telling me that Debbie was dead; beautiful, fun-loving, full-of-life Debbie had been killed in an accident.

I went to pieces. I screamed. I pounded my fists against the door. I asked God why? Why my baby again? Jesus please help me!

At that moment Dusty walked into the room, having just returned from the church. He said nothing at first, just grabbed me and shook me.

Finally he spoke. "Mom, for as long as I can remember you've been telling me to trust Jesus. If you meant that—and I think you did—you had better start trusting him right now. Debbie is okay. She's with him."

If I live to be a hundred I doubt I'll ever get any better advice than my son gave me at that moment.

The doctor arrived shortly and gave me something to settle my nerves, and I began to regain some composure. I went looking for little Dodie and found her out back, huddled with the dogs, crying her eyes out.

We had a good cry together, and went into the house. I placed a call to Art Rush, telling him to make sure Roy didn't hear the news on the radio or television. As always, he was several steps ahead of me, at the hospital, and had persuaded the members of the press not to release anything about Debbie's death until I had been told.

I felt as if I were walking around in a trance. Even when the coroner in San Diego called to tell me that Bob Russell, Joanne's father, had identified Debbie's and Joanne's bodies, I held to the hope that it was all a mistake, a bad dream from which I would somehow wake.

It was no dream, no mistake. We soon got the story of how it had happened.

On the trip home Debbie and Joanne had been standing up at the front of the bus and talking with Larry White, who was driving, when the left front tire blew. The blow-out sent the bus, weighted with sixty-six passengers, spinning uncontrollably into the oncoming traffic. A station wagon had run head-on into the bus.

Someone at the accident scene later said it was a miracle that no more lives were lost. In addition to Debbie and Joanne, six occupants of the station wagon were killed.

IT HAD FALLEN to Roy's surgeon to break the news to him. And then I talked with him briefly on the phone. Neither of us could say much. I don't believe I ever saw him take anything harder. A beautifully sentimental man, never afraid to show his emotions, he had shown amazing strength when his first wife died. And when Robin passed away it had been left to him to take care of all the funeral arrangements and lend me part of his strength to get through the ordeal. In 1958, when his beloved mother had died, it had been Roy who provided the shoulder for everyone to cry on.

The news of Debbie's death, however, was such a traumatic jolt that the doctors immediately ordered him returned to the hospital intensive care unit. This time, I realized, the trip to Forest Lawn to make funeral arrangements would be mine.

The following day I went first to visit Roy at the UCLA Medical Center, and then went to make arrangements for the double funeral. The Russell's other daughter, Kathy, had been injured, and they were with her in the hospital at Oceanside. I picked out two caskets and flowers, and made the arrangements for the services. This time the closed casket was not my decision, but that of the coroner. The attendant at Forest Lawn explained to me that the coroner had advised that the casket not be opened under any circumstances.

I agreed, partially. Since Robin's death I had lived with the regret of not having looked at her in death. I did not allow myself the same mistake with Debbie. I looked down at her, dressed in her pink sixth grade graduation dress, her little hands clasping a little blue stuffed animal she had won at the Ocean Park amusement center on her birthday. And I fell to my knees and thanked God for the nine years he had allowed us to have that beautiful little girl.

The next morning the entire family decided to dress for the service just as we had dressed for Debbie's sixth grade commencement. Dodie wore white, and I wore a pink dress and a short veil. The boys dressed in what they referred to as their Sunday suits.

Before we left, I prayed for the strength to be a good Christian witness during the service. Then I went into the garden and picked the three prettiest rosebuds I could find to place in Debbie's hands. I also called ahead to ask that one of the attendants see to it that a new gold cross was placed around her neck to replace the one which had been lost in the accident.

The Reverend Ralph Hoopes, minister of the Valley Presbyterian Church, a long-time friend and a wonderful man of God, conducted the service—Larry was still hospitalized. Larry's wife, however, represented the Chapel beautifully with a short eulogy to Debbie and Joanne, and the Reverend Leonard Eilers offered a prayer.

There were friends and loved ones everywhere. Floral arrangements came from all over the country, along with heartwarming cards and telegrams and letters. And then it was over.

At least I thought it was. A week after the funeral I went into Debbie's room, thinking it time to go through her closet and decide what to do about her things. Standing there, looking at all those lovely clothes she would never again wear, all the agony and pain came flooding back. I rushed to the kitchen, crying, saying aloud that it wasn't fair, that I could not understand why something like this could have been allowed to happen to my little girl.

In the midst of my tirade, I turned to see my mother standing in the doorway, glaring at me in a manner only mothers can do. She had come on the first plane from Texas as soon as I called her with the news of Debbie's death and had remained, offering support and sympathy throughout the ordeal. Now, however, there was neither support nor sympathy in her eyes. "I'm surprised at you," she scolded. "And disappointed. You know better than to give way to this. What has happened to your faith?"

For the second time in just a matter of days I had wavered, but had the good fortune to have members of my family standing by to set me straight—first Dusty, then my mother.

SHORTLY AFTER THE FUNERAL Dale Evans began to write her own moving tribute to her daughter. For days she wrote obsessively, much as she had done twelve years earlier following Robin's death, filling page after page with warm reflections, with love, and with Christian candor. The book would be entitled Dearest Debbie, and its royalties were to be donated to World Vision, Inc., the organization which, with the help of Dr. Bob Pierce, had made it possible for Deborah Lee Rogers to come from Korea to the United States.

And even as Dale wrote her book, there was yet another tragic footnote to the soul-trying episode. Roy, deeply affected by the death of Debbie, was finally dismissed from the hospital and allowed to return to the Double R Ranch. Wearing a neck brace, he was told to avoid any activity for a while. Thus it was that he was resting in bed one afternoon a couple of weeks after the funeral when the son of the Rogers' gardener came to the house with disturbing news and a frightened look on his face.

Shortly after the funeral, Bob Russell, the father of Debbie's friend Joanne, had disappeared. At first his wife, aware of his despair over the loss of their daughter, assumed that he had decided to drive back East to spend a few days with his parents. Days passed, however, and there was no word. Eventually a missing person report was filed, but to no avail.

Then on that sunny Sunday afternoon the young gardener's son, who was walking his dog near one of the barns considerably removed from the general path of activity at the ranch, noticed the sun reflecting on something shiny inside the closed building. Peeking inside, he saw a car, with what looked like a man seated motionless at the wheel.

He raced to the house to tell his father and Roy. The police were summoned, and upon their arrival found the body of Bob Russell. On the floorboard beneath his feet were several unused sleeping pills.

The coroner ruled the death a suicide.

"There are a lot of things that happen in this world," Roy would later say, "that I have to admit I don't understand. Maybe I'm not supposed to understand. I'm sure it was grief that drove Bob to do what he did, but he had so much to live for."

15

IT WAS TIME, ROY AND DALE agreed, to begin slowing the pace. They talked of retiring, of finding a place somewhere in the High Desert country where life would be less hectic.

"There are some people who, having spent most of their lives in show business, find that regardless of their age they simply cannot survive without it. Bob Hope is like that. And it's no criticism of Bob. But I was never that much of an extrovert. It was—and still is—hard for me to perform, to get up *in front of people. I enjoy it, but it isn't something that has ever come easy.*

"When the movies and television series came to an end, I was ready. I had had enough of it. And it seemed to me that Westerns could use a rest, too, since television was surfeited with horse operas."

It is perhaps necessary to offer up here the Roy Rogers–Dale Evans definition of retirement, lest anyone get the idea they had designs on his-and-her rocking chairs and keeping up with the daily happenings of "As The World Turns." Retirement to them was nothing more than a more selective approach to their work. There would be fewer *state fair appearances,* fewer *television specials,* fewer *recording sessions.*

Complete, hands down, cold turkey retirement is no more possible for the King of the Cowboys and the Queen of the West than it is for Bob Hope. If nothing else, there is the public demand. "One of the things I never learned to do very well," admits Roy, "is say no. And, you know, there have been precious few times that I've regretted that particular shortcoming."

I HAD PROMISED NEVER TO TELL my barlow knife story again once the children were all raised and gone. Not that it isn't a good story and one with a message. Dale says I just overused it a little. Looking back, I would have to say her judgment is an understatement.

It got to the point, in fact, that I would launch into it, dead set on making my point, and would get one of those patient "here it comes again" looks. It finally became so amusing to Dale that she would have to take quick leave of the room so that her amusement would not hamper the serious tone I was trying to set.

As the children grew up, it always concerned me that they lacked the proper degree of appreciation for material things. There were always plenty of presents at Christmas and on birthdays. Financial hard times were never really a part of their growing-up experience.

And so, when Christmas presents would be too quickly discarded or torn up, I would tell them the story of the Christmas

Dad gave me this pocket knife. That was all I got, but it was one of the greatest treasures I ever owned. I took care of it, I polished it, I guarded it like a fine piece of jewelry.

I told that story when the girls would rip rampantly through all their presents on Christmas morning. I told it when Dusty and Sandy took the motor out of their go-cart and dismantled it. I told it when Dusty complained that most of the kids at high school were driving far newer cars than he was. I told it prior to birthdays when they asked for expensive gifts. I told it, I guess, until it took its place right alongside the old "I had to walk five miles to school in the snow every day—uphill all the way" story. But I told it with a purpose and, looking back, I like to think I got my point over.

Now that I think about it, Sandy was probably my best audience. Having come to us with nothing but a tattered little sweater stuffed into a grocery bag, I think he understood what I was saying. Not that he always agreed, mind you; but he understood.

In January of 1965, we were making plans to move to Apple Valley near Victorville. One evening as Dale and I sat discussing the move, Sandy came in and asked if he could talk with us. Clearly, he had something of a serious nature on his mind.

And it was quickly obvious that his presentation had been well prepared. "I'm not making good grades in high school," he pointed out, "so what I'd like to do is enlist in the army. That's what I want to do more than anything else in the world. I think I can prove myself as a soldier.

"I'll be eighteen in June," he continued, "and I could wait until then, but I would like to go now if you will give me the permission. I promise that I'll get my high school diploma in the service. And I promise that I'll make you proud of me."

The latter he had already done, time and time again. Despite the hardships dealt him in infancy, John David (Sandy) Rogers had never been a quitter. As he grew older, he recognized his limitations in certain areas, but he never let those stop him. He and Dusty loved to wrestle, and if Sandy ever won I wasn't aware of it, but he always came back for more. He tried out for Little League summer after summer but never made the team. So he served as an enthusiastic and hard-working bat boy while the others enjoyed the glories of hitting home runs and seeing their names in the local paper.

He made a concerted effort in the remedial reading classes to which we sent him, but with only marginal success. As many hours as I worked with him, he could never master a shotgun at the trap-shooting range. But he never let disappointment or discouragement show. Rather, he would mask it behind a clown face, going into an elaborate comedy routine in his moments of shortcoming, and then come back for more.

There are those, I'm sure, who will tell you that Sandy didn't have much going for him. The truth of the matter is he had a great deal going for him. Call it fatherly boasting if you will, but I've met few people in my life with more heart than Sandy.

And so we agreed to let him enlist, secretly feeling that his chances of passing the physical examination were slim.

Dale and I, of course, had mixed emotions. If he failed the exam that would mean he would stay at home, and would finish his final year of high school. On the other hand, if he was not allowed to enlist, a life's dream would be shattered. From his first days at the military academy, Sandy had been fascinated, almost obsessed, with the service. When he was sixteen, he and Dusty had gotten summer jobs digging ditches and, saving his money, Sandy wound up spending all of his earnings at the Army Surplus Store in Canoga Park to purchase an old Civil War sword, which he cherished every bit as much as I did the aforementioned pocket knife.

Thus it was with a mixture of sorrow and pride that we learned he had passed his physical. We signed his release and saw him off to Fort Polk, where he was to go through basic training.

He went off to serve his country, and we went off to Apple Valley.

THE DAY SANDY GRADUATED from basic training at Fort Polk, Louisiana, was one of the biggest of his life. He immediately volunteered for duty in Viet Nam, but instead was sent to Fort Leonard Wood in Missouri.

He did get a short leave and came home for a few days, but we saw very little of him. He was far more interested in a young lady named Sharyn, whom he had been dating steadily before enlisting. Before leaving, he broke the news to us that they had decided to become engaged. He had also made the decision that he wanted to pursue a military career.

At Fort Leonard Wood, he volunteered for demolition squad duty, one of the most hazardous jobs offered, but was turned down. Transferred to Fort Knox, he again requested assignment in Viet Nam. Again his request was denied. While he was never given a detailed reason, Dale and I later had it explained to us: The guerrilla warfare going on in Viet Nam demanded that a soldier be able to think quickly and react quickly. These abilities Sandy, through no fault of his own, lacked.

Thus his next stop would be Germany.

Dale flew to Fort Knox to say good-bye, and returned home disturbed over an admission Sandy made to her before she left. On his eighteenth birthday, he told her, he had participated in a beer bust with several of his friends. Clearly he felt badly about doing so, Dale said, but she was unable to pass it off as a boys-will-be-boys fling. His parents, we both knew, had been alcoholics, and Dale voiced her concern that he might have inherited a weakness for alcohol.

I did my best to convince her that she was worrying over nothing. It would be Sandy himself, however, who set her mind at ease with a letter he wrote shortly after arriving in Germany:

Dear Mom and Dad:

I'll make this promise to both of you—that when Sharyn and I get married and raise our kids, they will be raised in a home where Christ is Lord. That old saying, "A family that prays together stays together," goes for both of us. We will try our hardest to raise our kids as God wants them to be raised. It's tough that I didn't finish high school in civilian life, but I'm going to finish it in the army, and I'll make you both, and everyone else, proud of me. I realize that it isn't much of a jump from being seventeen to being eighteen, but I have finally realized that parents aren't just talking to hear their heads rattle when they're trying to tell us something. All the time, kids think they're smart and their par-

ents are dumb, but it's just the opposite. Parents are the smart
ones and the kids are the dumb ones. Someday when I have
my own kids, I hope I can show them the patience that you've
shown me and the other kids.

> God bless you both always,
> Love, Sandy

Again in Germany he volunteered to go to Viet Nam but
instead remained there and, to my everlasting amazement, managed to get into the tank corps. I had underestimated him.
There he was, promoted to private first class, and in the driver's
seat of a military tank, when he had left home without even
benefit of a driver's license.

His letters home were a delight, filled with self-confidence
and a well-deserved touch of pride. Sandy was happier than
he had ever been in his life, and Dale and I delighted in his
joy.

On the homefront things were progressing nicely. Dusty was
in his senior year at Victorville High School, and Dodie was
in the eighth grade. She, Dale, and I were attending the Presbyterian Church of the Valley, while Dusty had chosen to attend
the High Desert Baptist Church where many of his school
friends were members.

In late October of that year, Dale decided to make a trip
home to celebrate her birthday with her mother. Having long
since dismissed her fear of flying, she was eagerly looking
forward to going to Texas. I suppose, in fact, if I keep her in
California until she's one hundred and twenty-five, she'll still
refer to Texas as "home."

Going to Italy was always an event for Dale. Elaborate plans
had been made for her to sing in the church choir on Sunday
and to give her testimony to the congregation. Then, in the
company of her mother and other family members, she would
drive to nearby Waxahachie for her birthday dinner.

I only wish her celebration could have lasted longer. The
night before she was to return home tragedy struck, as it always
does, in a moment when least expected. The call had come
to our house: Pfc. Sandy Rogers, age eighteen, a fine soldier,
was dead.

A look of horror wiped the smile from Dale's face the moment she stepped from the plane. Marion had planned to meet her, have coffee, and bring her home. Instead, we were all there as a family. Dale knew immediately something was wrong.

It was Cheryl who reached her first. "Is there a problem?" her mother asked. No hugs, no kisses, no warm hello. Somehow she seemed to know already.

"It's Sandy," Cheryl said. "He's gone."

It made no more sense to her than it had to me. Sandy was not in the battlefields of Viet Nam. He was in Germany, far removed from the conflict. How could he be gone? How could still another of our children be dead even before he had had a chance to live?

Gently, Dusty took his mother by the arm, and in a manner which far belied his age, explained the bare details for her. "Sandy was at a party Saturday night," he told her, "and some of the guys talked him into drinking a lot of hard liquor and it killed him, Mom. I'm sorry."

Dale buried her face in her hands and sobbed. She said nothing, just cried silently while the rest of us stood by, feeling helpless, empty. Sandy's death was senseless, without rhyme or proper reason. If there are degrees of tragedy, his passing was one of the highest order.

He had returned from twenty-six days of grueling maneuvers, dog-tired and glad they were over. Several of his friends had suggested that a celebration was in order, inasmuch as Sandy had not, in the military tradition, "wet down his stripes" since attaining the rank of Pfc.

They had showered, dressed, picked up their pay, and gone to the enlistment men's club for dinner. Then he had been challenged: "You're a man now, Rogers; let's see if you can drink like one."

I can see him now, that crazy grin on his face, eager to prove himself, eager to be accepted, a part. It wasn't any different from what he had been doing all his life. And, bless him, he fell for the challenge.

In a short period of time he had drunk a half bottle of champagne, two beers, four mixtures of whiskey, gin, vodka,

and brandy, and a sweet cordial. And collapsed, unconscious.

His companions, realizing that this young man who had
never tasted anything stronger than beer had gone far beyond
any reasonable limits, had tried to revive him and then had
taken him, on their shoulders, to the dispensary. The orderly,
instead of pumping his stomach, had put him into his bunk
to sleep it off. The following morning, the same day his mother
was singing in the Baptist church in Italy, Texas, they had
found him dead.

When told the story I had gone into an emotional tailspin.
I was grief-stricken by the loss of a son who had battled so
gallantly to find his place in life, and I was bitterly angry at a
society which could pressure a person to such a meaningless
waste. For Dale and me both, the tears and sorrow were not
so much for ourselves and our loss, as for the loss Sandy
had suffered, for the unfulfilled dreams, the hopes which would
not be realized, the plans that would not be carried out.

We waited for his body to be flown home. He would have
a full military funeral and then be laid to rest in a crypt at
Forest Lawn next to Robin and Debbie. The services were
brief. Taps was played and a salute cracked from the rifles
of the military escort on hand. The American flag, for which
Sandy had wanted so badly to fight, to defend in battle in
Viet Nam, was taken from the casket, folded, and handed to
Dale.

Watching as his friends stood silently by, bidding him farewell, paying their last respects; as Dale proudly and coura-
geously accepted the traditional flag, I felt all the strength go
out of my body. And I cried. That lonely-sad-happy-mischie-
vous-beautiful little boy from Kentucky who, just a few short
years earlier, had looked up at me for the first time, shaken
my hand, and said, "Howdy pad-nuh," a little guy I had loved
the minute I saw him, was gone.

Dale reached over and touched my arm. "Honey," she whispered, "Sandy's with God . . . and Debbie and Robin." It was
a comforting thought. Still, I was going to miss him. We all
would.

Just before Christmas that year, a package came in the mail

from Sandy's commanding officer in Germany. In it were the wedding and engagement rings he had purchased for Sharyn. We gave them to her, and she had them made into a cross, a gesture Sandy would have liked.

He also would have liked the bronze plaque which now stands between a big, beautiful tree and a singing water fountain on the grounds of the Chapel in the Canyon. The inscription describes him well:

John David (Sandy) Rogers
Here he played. Here he prayed.
Here he loved, and was loved by all.

That summer Dale and I were asked by the USO to do an entertainment tour of Viet Nam. We accepted for several reasons. Perhaps by going we might in some way help Sandy to fulfill his desire to be there. And, too, we wanted to see firsthand what this seemingly unpopular conflict our soldiers were involved in was all about. And Dale had talked to her editor about writing a book about Sandy, and hoped to talk to some of his army buddies about his brief life as a soldier.

Frankly, I began the trip with some reservations. I wasn't sure what to expect. All I knew was that it would be unlike any of the hundreds of USO tours we had done in the States years earlier. The spirit of Sandy would ride along on this trip. There would be Sandys at every stop along the way—young men who fully realized there were those back home who made no pretense of supporting what they were doing. I wondered what their reaction would be to our visit. And I wondered, too, what our reaction would be to them.

It pleases me greatly to report that what we found was the finest example of American youth you could ever hope to see. We saw a strong, unbending dedication to a necessary task. We saw suffering, but heard no complaining. We saw courage and faith and a patriotic dedication to doing a job that they felt, knew had to be done.

We came home believing in those soldiers and in their cause.

And we also brought with us some heart-warming reflections of our son. One of Sandy's friends gave us a Vietnamese picture on which he had written "In Memory of John." The captain of his outfit at Fort Polk had told Dale that in his eighteen years of service experience he had never known a young man so anxious to be a soldier, had never seen one who tried so hard. A sergeant who had had no idea of Sandy's difficulties said, "There were times when I got so mad at him I wanted to choke him until his eyes popped out. He would make a mistake and go into that crazy comedy routine. But he stayed after it, never gave up. You can't help but admire that. I just wish I had known a little more about him."

It sounded to me like he knew plenty.

We came home spiritually uplifted but physically exhausted. All I wanted to do was sleep, but Dale, working diligently to complete the book she had worked on throughout our trip, didn't slow a bit.

On what would have been Sandy's nineteenth birthday, *Salute to Sandy,* the story of our son and our travels to Viet Nam, was published, and Dale arranged to have the royalties paid to the Campus Crusade for Christ International.

Sandy would also have liked that.

As with all the tragedies which have befallen the Rogers family, their mourning was shared by people throughout the nation, the world. Long after Sandy's death, letters of sympathy continued to arrive. Some carried simple messages of condolence, others words of admiration for the strength and faith maintained by Roy and Dale through their trying ordeals. And with the publication of each new book by Dale, there would come a steady stream of testimonies, indications that she, by telling of the manner in which she and her family had dealt with shock and sorrow, had helped others deal with similar situations.

And, as Roy is so fond of saying, for every sorrow in his life there have been a thousand joys.

Shortly after graduation Dusty, eager to have his crack at making it in the world, moved to Middlefield, Ohio, where he went to work in a supermarket with a close friend named George White whose father owned the business. There was the expected urging on the part of his parents to stay a bit closer to home, but the final decision was properly left to Dusty. He had earned the right to make it. Being Roy Rogers, Jr., is not the easiest assignment a young man can draw, but he had handled it well.

Roy and Dale respected his decision and bade him godspeed. It was not long before they too were summoned to Middlefield, to attend the wedding of their son and a beautiful young girl named Linda Yoder. Predictably, Dad beamed and Mom shed a few tears and both realized there would be yet another empty bedroom back home.

There was only Dodie, still young but fast approaching the time when she, too, would no doubt go away to make a life of her own. She served as a bridesmaid at Dusty's wedding. Then, in the fall of 1969, she became the bride of an Air Force staff sergeant. She was the last of the flock to leave.

When the wedding festivities were over, they returned to a quiet house. Dale cried again, and Roy put his arm around her. "Honey," he said, "it's not as if we don't have kids anymore. We've got grandchildren running out our ears, and there's no telling how many more to come. I suspect they're going to keep us pretty busy."

Dale smiled. "I suspect they will," she said.

Epilogue

CLEARLY, THE STORY of Roy Rogers and Dale Evans is far from ending. Their retirement, in fact, may be one of the busiest ever undertaken.

Roy and Dale continue to establish new all-time box-office records at state fairs and rodeos, and hardly a month goes by that television viewers don't see them as guest stars on everything from "The Muppet Show" to "Hee Haw" to Christmas specials and talk shows.

The number of books written by Dale now totals seventeen, with a combined total of over four million copies sold. Roy is actively involved in over two hundred Marriott Corporation-owned Roy Rogers Family Restaurants throughout the United States and Canada. While he travels to openings of new restaurants, often accompanied by Dusty and the Sons of the Pioneers, Dale takes her moving message of faith to concerts and Christian rallies all over the country.

And there is the Roy Rogers–Dale Evans Museum in Victorville, to which thousands come annually to view the artifacts of one of the entertainment world's most well-known families. It is a warm, fascinating collection of photographs, show business memorabilia, family mementoes, citations, and treasured gifts certain to bring back fond memories to any of yesteryear's Saturday Afternoon Deputies who once lent support to the King of the Cowboys and the Queen of the West from a front-row vantage point down at the Bijou. Trigger, who died in 1965, is there, beautifully mounted. So is Trigger, Jr., Buttermilk, Bullet, and even Pat Brady's jeep Nellybelle.

When not traveling or taping a TV show or adding to the list of over four hundred songs they have recorded or greeting visitors to the museum, Roy, showing no ill effects of the bypass surgery he underwent in 1978, spends a lot of time on his sixty-seven acre thoroughbred ranch or at the Victor Lanes bowling alley where he maintains an 180 average in league play. Or out in the desert with his favorite bird dog, Sam. Or at a nearby gun club, still shooting trap and skeet as well as most men half his age.

And there is always time for frequent visits from all the grand-children and great-grandchildren; the Rogers clan has increased rather than dwindled with passing years.

What those children have inherited is a legacy they share with an entire nation. Roy and Dale's kinship to millions of people whose names and faces they don't even know is as real as any family ties will ever be. Roy and Dale continue to be loved and admired in a way that few, if any, celebrities can claim.

That affection is not only for what they are and who they are, but for what they represent. In a time when heroes are in short supply, Roy Rogers remains one—a man who flaunts no macho image and waves no celestial bankrolls, but instead simply lives the good life, standing firm in his beliefs and main-taining a close rein on his priorities. Dale Evans represents proof positive that the roles of mother-wife-career woman can be successfully woven. Together, they stand as a solid example of what the family unit is supposed to be and as a steadfast witness to the faith that has sustained them.

A legacy indeed! It is an example that any child—or any nation—would do well to follow.

Filmography

The following is a list of the Republic Studios films in which Roy Rogers starred, along with a listing of principal supporting actors and actresses:

1938

Under Western Stars—Roy Rogers, Smiley Burnette, Carol Hughes, Guy Usher

Billy the Kid Returns—Roy Rogers, Smiley Burnette, Lynn Roberts, Morgan Wallace

Come On Rangers—Roy Rogers, Raymond Hatton, J. Farrell Mac-Donald, Mary Hart

Shine On Harvest Moon—Roy Rogers, Mary Hart, Stanley Andrews, William Farnum

Texas Legionnaires—Roy Rogers, Ruth Terry, George Cleveland, Paul Kelly

1939

Southward Ho—Roy Rogers, Gabby Hayes, Mary Hart, Wade Boteler

Rough Riders' Round-Up—Roy Rogers, Raymond Hatton, Eddie Acuff, Duncan Renaldo

Saga of Death Valley—Roy Rogers, Gabby Hayes, Don Barry, Frank M. Thomas

Frontier Pony Express—Roy Rogers, Raymond Hatton, Monte Blue, Mary Hart

In Old Caliente—Roy Rogers, Gabby Hayes, Katherine DeMille, Jack LaRue

Days of Jesse James—Roy Rogers, Gabby Hayes, Don Barry, Pauline Moore

Arizona Kid—Roy Rogers, Gabby Hayes, Sally March, Stuart Hamblen

Wall Street Cowboy—Roy Rogers, Gabby Hayes, Raymond Hatton, Ann Baldwin

1940

Young Buffalo Bill—Roy Rogers, Gabby Hayes, Pauline Moore, Hugh Southern

Young Bill Hickock—Roy Rogers, Gabby Hayes, Jacqueline Wells, Monte Blue

West of the Badlands—Roy Rogers, Gabby Hayes, Carol Hughes, Joseph Sawyer

Dark Command—John Wayne, Claire Trevor, Walter Pidgeon, Roy Rogers, Marjorie Main, Gabby Hayes

Carson City Kid—Roy Rogers, Gabby Hayes, Bob Steele, Noah Beery, Jr.

Colorado—Roy Rogers, Gabby Hayes, Pauline Moore, Milburn Stone

The Ranger and the Lady—Roy Rogers, Gabby Hayes, Henry Brandon, Jacqueline Wells

1941

Red River Valley—Roy Rogers, Gabby Hayes, Gale Storm, Sally Payne

Robin Hood of the Pecos—Roy Rogers, Gabby Hayes, Marjorie Reynolds, Cy Kendall

Sheriff of Tombstone—Roy Rogers, Gabby Hayes, Elyse Knox, Addison Richards

In Old Cheyenne—Roy Rogers, Gabby Hayes, Joan Woodbury, J. Farrell MacDonald

Jesse James at Bay—Roy Rogers, Gabby Hayes, Gale Storm, Sally Payne

Nevada City—Roy Rogers, Gabby Hayes, George Cleveland, Sally Payne

Bad Man of Deadwood—Roy Rogers, Gabby Hayes, Henry Brandon, Carol Adams

1942

Heart of the Golden West—Roy Rogers, Smiley Burnette, Gabby Hayes, Ruth Terry

Man from Cheyenne—Roy Rogers, Gabby Hayes, Gale Storm, Sally
    Payne
Ridin' Down the Canyon—Roy Rogers, Gabby Hayes, Linda Hayes,
    Addison Richards
Romance on the Range—Roy Rogers, Gabby Hayes, Sally Payne,
    Linda Hayes
Sons of the Pioneers—Roy Rogers, Gabby Hayes, Maris Wrixon,
    Forrest Taylor
South of Santa Fe—Roy Rogers, Gabby Hayes, Linda Hayes, Paul
    Fix
Sunset on the Desert—Roy Rogers, Gabby Hayes, Lynne Carver,
    Frank M. Thomas
Sunset Serenade—Roy Rogers, Gabby Hayes, Helen Parrish, Joan
    Woodbury

1943

Silver Spurs—Roy Rogers, Jerome Cowan, John Carradine, Smiley
    Burnette
Song of Texas—Roy Rogers, Trigger, Barton Maclane, Sheila Ryan
King of the Cowboys—Roy Rogers, Smiley Burnette, Peggy Moran,
    Gerald Mohr
Hands Across the Border—Roy Rogers, Ruth Terry, Duncan Renaldo,
    Guinn Williams
Idaho—Roy Rogers, Smiley Burnette, Virginia Grey, Harry Shannon

1944

Yellow Rose of Texas—Roy Rogers, Dale Evans, Grant Withers,
    George Cleveland
The Cowboy and the Senorita—Roy Rogers, Dale Evans, Fuzzy
    Knight, Guinn Williams
Lights of Old Santa Fe—Roy Rogers, Trigger, Dale Evans, Gabby
    Hayes
San Fernando Valley—Roy Rogers, Dale Evans, Edward Gargan,
    Jean Porter
Song of Nevada—Roy Rogers, Trigger, Dale Evans, Mary Lee

1945

Man from Oklahoma—Roy Rogers, Trigger, Gabby Hayes, Dale
    Evans
Along the Navajo Trail—Roy Rogers, Trigger, Dale Evans, Gabby
    Hayes, Estelita Rodriquez

Bells of Rosarita—Roy Rogers, Dale Evans, Gabby Hayes, Bill Elliott
Don't Fence Me In—Roy Rogers, Dale Evans, Gabby Hayes, Bob
      Livingston
Utah—Roy Rogers, Dale Evans, Gabby Hayes, Grant Withers
Sunset in El Dorado—Roy Rogers, Dale Evans, Gabby Hayes,
      Margaret DuMont

1946

Under Nevada Skies—Roy Rogers, Dale Evans, Gabby Hayes, Doug-
      lass Dumbrille
Heldorado—Roy Rogers, Dale Evans, Gabby Hayes, Paul Harvey
Home in Oklahoma—Roy Rogers, Dale Evans, Gabby Hayes, Carol
      Hughes
My Pal Trigger—Roy Rogers, Dale Evans, Gabby Hayes, Jack
      Holt
Rainbow over Texas—Roy Rogers, Dale Evans, Gabby Hayes, Shel-
      don Leonard
Roll On Texas Moon—Roy Rogers, Trigger, Dale Evans, Gabby Hayes
Song of Arizona—Roy Rogers, Trigger, Dale Evans, Gabby Hayes

1947

On the Old Spanish Trail—Roy Rogers, Andy Devine, Jane Frazee,
      Tito Guizar
Apache Rose—Roy Rogers, Trigger, Dale Evans, George Meeker
Bells of San Angelo—Roy Rogers, Trigger, Dale Evans, Andy Devine
Springtime in the Sierras—Roy Rogers, Trigger, Andy Devine, Jane
      Frazee

1948

Under California Stars—Roy Rogers, Trigger, Andy Devine, Jane
      Frazee
Eyes of Texas—Roy Rogers, Trigger, Andy Devine, Francis Ford
The Far Frontier—Roy Rogers, Andy Devine, Clayton Moore, Gail
      Davis
Grand Canyon Trail—Roy Rogers, Trigger, Andy Devine, Jane Frazee
Nighttime in Nevada—Roy Rogers, Andy Devine, Adele Mara, Grant
      Withers

1949

Susanna Pass—Roy Rogers, Trigger, Dale Evans, Estelita Rodriguez

Down Dakota Way—Roy Rogers, Dale Evans, Roy Barcroft, Montie
        Montana
The Golden Stallion—Roy Rogers, Dale Evans, Estelita Rodriguez,
        Pat Brady

1950

Trail of Robin Hood—Roy Rogers, Rex Allen, Allan Lane, Monte
        Hale
Trigger, Jr.—Roy Rogers, Trigger, Dale Evans, Pat Brady
Twilight in the Sierras—Roy Rogers, Dale Evans, Pat Brady, Estelita
        Rodriguez
Sunset in the West—Roy Rogers, Trigger, Penny Edwards, Estelita
        Rodriguez
Bells of Coronado—Roy Rogers, Dale Evans, Pat Brady, Grant
        Withers
North of the Great Divide—Roy Rogers, Trigger, Penny Edwards,
        Gordon Jones

1951

Pals of the Golden West—Roy Rogers, Trigger, Dale Evans, Estelita
        Rodriguez
Heart of the Rockies—Roy Rogers, Trigger, Penny Edwards, Ralph
        Morgan
In Old Amarillo—Roy Rogers, Estelita Rodriguez, Penny Edwards,
        Pinky Lee
Spoilers of the Plains—Roy Rogers, Trigger, Penny Edwards, Grant
        Withers
South of Caliente—Roy Rogers, Dale Evans, Pinky Lee, Pat Brady

1952

The Gay Ranchero—Roy Rogers, Trigger, Jane Frazee, Andy Devine

Following his fourteen-year career with Republic Studios, Roy Rogers
had star billing in two later motion pictures, in addition to the 101
episodes of his television series:

1952

Son of Paleface (Paramount)—Bob Hope, Jane Russell, Roy Rogers,
        Bill Williams

1976

Mackintosh and T. J. (Penland Productions)—Roy Rogers, Clay
O'Brien,   Joan
Hackett,   Walter
Barnes